# A Thousand Waves

Also by David K. Reynolds

*Playing Ball on Running Water*
*Even in Summer the Ice Doesn't Melt*
*Water Bears No Scars*
*Pools of Lodging for the Moon*

# A Thousand

## DAVID K. REYNOLDS
### PH.D.

# *Waves*

A Sensible Life Style
for Sensitive People

QUILL
WILLIAM MORROW
NEW YORK

Recognizing the importance of preserving what has been written, it is the policy of William Morrow and Company, Inc., and its imprints and affiliates to have the books it publishes printed on acid-free paper, and we exert our best efforts to that end.

Library of Congress Cataloging-in-Publication Data

Reynolds, David K.
  A thousand waves : a sensible life style for sensitive people /
David K. Reynolds.
    p.   cm.
  Includes bibliographical references
  ISBN 0–688–08157–6 / 0–688–09434-1 (pbk)
    1. Morita psychotherapy. 2. Naikan psychotherapy. 3. Mental health. I. Title.
RC489.M65R46   1990
616.89'14—dc20                                                     89-14284
                                                                       CIP

Printed in the United States of America


    2   3   4   5   6   7   8   9   10

BOOK DESIGN BY JAYE ZIMET

To Lynn Sanae Reynolds;
to Brian, Said, Patricia, Gregg,
and all my students/teachers

# Acknowledgments

I have worked hard at presenting in my writings a lifeway that would attract attention because of its unique qualities, its originality. But the more I live, read, and listen, the more I encounter only slightly differing versions of constructive living from many lands and many times. Life wisdom is life wisdom. What works, works. What lasts, lasts. What is passed on from generation to generation merits our attention. You will read in this book just another formulation of this life wisdom that has been passed on for safekeeping.

Many of these truths were filtered through the life experiences and teaching of Yozo Hasegawa Sensei and the members of Hakkenkai, the lay organization of Moritists in Japan. Dr. Hiromu Shimbo and his wife, Rev. Ishin Yoshimoto and his wife, Rev. Shue Usami and his wife, Dr. Takezo Ishii, Mr. Mitsuto Saito, Mrs. Suzuyo Otani, and Dr. F. Ishu Ishiyama taught me about this lifeway by word and example. The writings and conversations of three psychiatrists—Dr. Takehisa Kora, Dr. Tomonori Suzuki, and Dr. Kenshiro Ohara—have been influential in my understanding of this lifeway. Professor Mori and Dr. Kitanishi of Jikei University Medical School, where Morita himself was professor, provided support and encouragement during the recent years of my studies and a welcome to many visiting Westerners.

In the United States the Shigetada Tamashiro family, Dr. and Mrs. Mamoru Iga, Dr. and Mrs. Brian Ogawa, and my constructive-living students all gave me life instruction in this path.

Gratitude waxes and wanes; it is, after all, a feeling. An acknowledgment of appreciation is behavior. It is a pleasure to acknowledge my debt to these teachers in print.

The times when they taught and I didn't listen or look, when the lesson was there but my mind was somewhere else, when I distorted the wisdom to fit my private needs, when I did less than the best I could do—I apologize and take responsibility for the errors.

My research in Japan was funded, in part, by the Mental Health Okamoto Memorial Foundation. This foundation has made a genuine, positive impact on the development of Morita therapy and Naikan in Japan.

Douglas Stumpf, my editor at William Morrow (ably assisted these days by Jared Stamm), continues to support the publication of the Constructive Living series. *Playing Ball on Running Water, Even in Summer the Ice Doesn't Melt, Water Bears No Scars,* and *Pools of Lodging for the Moon* are earlier titles in that series.

# Contents

Trying to subdue a wave by striking it only results in a thousand waves

—MORITA MASATAKE

# Introduction

The title of this book, like many of the ideas within it, comes from the Zen-inspired writings of the Japanese psychiatrist Morita Masatake (or Morita Shoma, depending on how one reads the Chinese characters of his given name). In this case he borrowed a Zen saying and gave it his characteristic twist. The original saying suggests that from a single ripple of desire grow thousands and tens of thousands of desires. Morita used the same saying to point out that as we try to suppress one feeling (the feeling of shyness or anxiety, for example), we only succeed in generating a thousand other feelings (worries about how successful we are at suppressing the discomfort, how long the success will last, what kind of people we are who need to go to such extremes to make life bearable, and so forth). Trying to suppress feelings (or create them) directly turns out to be as hopeless as trying to demolish a wave with a blow. Try it and see. This truth is part of the accumulation of human wisdom.

A major part of my life has been invested in describing an ocean of human wisdom with shores on every land. I have painted some scenes from that ocean as seen from Japanese shores. But the ocean doesn't belong to the Japanese. The same waves come lapping up to refresh and renew inhabitants of California mental hospitals, survivors of disasters across America, those who work with the dying and those who lie in V.A. hospital beds preparing to die, the experienced elderly and the wizened young. These waters nourish and cool. I have seen it do its work in these settings.

Often I missed the ocean views until they were pointed out by some kind dweller in that setting, often pointed out by gesture rather than by eloquent verbal description. Many have clear eyes to see at least part of their nearby seascape  Many know paths down to the water's edge. Usually, I merely followed along behind them. Reality provides so many teachers.

I don't write of military glory or national honor or grand economic victory or regal romance. My books are about the way to dial a phone or set a table or wash a dog, about a dustcloth, an eraser, a toothbrush, about a belt, a button, a shoelace—things I know something about. We'll consider the nobility and service and sacrifice of a doorknob, the glory of a window sash, the honor of a napkin holder, the grand soap dish. Does such writing seem ridiculous to you?

When I write a book or give a lecture or offer a short workshop, I don't hope to give you a solid grounding in constructive living. There just isn't enough time for the experiences necessary to learn this lifeway. The best I can hope for is to shake up some of your taken-for-granted assumptions about the human mind and human life and to make you uncomfortable and intrigued. Then some of you will come for further training, or at least you may try constructive-living exercises on your own.

Being uncomfortable in this situation is terrific. You can demonstrate to yourself that you can be uncomfortable and read on. You can be uncomfortable and try the exercises. The discomfort doesn't necessarily stop you from doing what you have decided needs doing. You have (re)learned an important lesson of constructive living: Feelings don't determine what we do.

Come, wade in this tidal basin from the ocean of human wisdom. It is no more mine than it is Japanese. It has evolved along the tangent between the human mind and reality. It is best appreciated up close—seen, felt, heard, smelled, tasted. From a distance the view is striking, but even a moment's immersion is absolutely indescribable.

# PART I

## CONSTRUCTIVE-LIVING ESSAYS

Discussing constructive living and thinking about it are of no benefit without practice. However talking, writing, and thinking can be part of the practice . . . provided we don't take those pursuits for the whole of it.

# Being Ordinary

*(In slightly revised form this chapter appeared in Sheikh, A. and Sheikh, K. Eastern Approaches to Mental Health. New York: Wiley, 1989.)*

Let's consider for a moment the quality of being ordinary. We fear that we *aren't* ordinary enough—that we are neurotic or overly shy or timid or suffering more than most people. And we fear that we *are* too ordinary—that we aren't superior, that we don't live up to our potential, that we fail to show our best qualities to others. These fears—the fear of not being ordinary enough and the fear of being too ordinary—are, of course, perfectly ordinary. We worry about the peculiarity of fears that are perfectly ordinary. What makes Woody Allen particularly funny is that we see our own self-doubts and anxieties reflected in his exaggerated performance of the ordinary.

Zen Buddhist masters have said that everyone is already a Buddha; we simply fail to recognize it. This chapter aims at describing the ways we are already ordinary, natural, just fine as we are, even though we may not have been aware of our present perfection.

Water is a symbol of the natural. By just naturally doing its thing, by just going about its water business in a waterlike way, it accomplishes all sorts of feats. Not the least of its accomplishments is its ability to provide us with analogies that help make sense of human psychology and provide advice for successful living.

Most of my recent books have water in the title: *Playing Ball on Running Water; Even in Summer the Ice Doesn't Melt; Water Bears No Scars; Pools of Lodging for the Moon;* and *Flowing Bridges, Quiet Waters* among others. The titles are taken from Zen koans or Zen-inspired poetry. In order, they refer, in part, to action in everchanging time, the chill stiffness of neurosis, the purposeful now-centeredness of water, the ability of the moon to find a resting place in a hundred bowls of water without making reservations or receiving invitations, and the subjective nature of situational changes.

The Eastern approaches to mental health that form what we call in the West constructive living are Morita therapy and Naikan therapy. They aim at helping us be natural. Some people believe that modern technology and other aspects of modern life have alienated us from nature. What does it mean to become natural again?

Let's begin with a look at how water is natural. First, water accepts the reality of the situation it is in. It doesn't say, "Now I'm in a glass, but I want to be in the ocean, so I'll sulk and daydream and not act like proper water." Only people do that. Water reflects whatever reality brings it.


> Tozan came to see Zen master Zehne of Kassan, and asked:
> "How are things?"
> "Just as they are."*

*Shibayama, 1970, p. 206

DAVID K. REYNOLDS

In warm times water becomes warm, in cold times it becomes cold. It doesn't say, "I wish I were cool today. I shouldn't get this hot." It doesn't pretend it is warm when it is really cold. It simply accepts the reality of its temperature and goes about flowing toward the lowest place around.

People deny reality. They fight against real feelings caused by real circumstances. They build mental worlds of shoulds, oughts, and might-have-beens. Real changes begin with real appraisal and acceptance of what is. Then realistic action is possible.

Water flows around obstacles. It doesn't stop on its way down a riverbed to try to fight with the big rocks that oppose it. It just heads toward its goal and eventually wears down its opposition. Whether the obstacles wear down quickly or not, water manages to get where it aims to go without any long-term distraction. People tend to get distracted by feelings (for example, by anxiety before college exams) and shift away from their original purposes (for example, by trying to resolve the anxiety instead of continuing to study for the exams).

Water is wonderfully flexible. It fills the circumstances it is in. It takes the natural amount of time to get where it is going. It moves at a natural pace—now rushing quickly, now flowing slowly, depending on the circumstances. Some people seem to be rushing around all the time, trying to force time to fit their desires. Other people never seem to stir themselves to fast action.

What is so outstanding about these qualities? They are just the ordinary qualities of water. This chapter is about being ordinary and natural human beings in much the same way, and about the trouble we get ourselves into when we aren't realistic in the sense that water is realistic.

## CONSTRUCTIVE LIVING

Constructive living is a bringing together of two psychotherapies and their associated lifeways with origins in Japan. As noted above, the two systems of dealing with human suffering and human existence are usually called Morita therapy and Naikan therapy. Both were developed in this century, but their roots extend back for hundreds of years into the history of east Asia. Morita was a professor of psychiatry at Jikei University School of Medicine in Tokyo. Yoshimoto was a successful businessman who retired to become a lay priest in Nara. Morita's method has its origins in Zen Buddhist psychology (not Zen Buddhist religion), and Yoshimoto's Naikan has its origins in Jodo Shinshu Buddhist psychology. Neither of these systems requires that one believe in Buddhism or have faith in anything other than one's own experience. They work as well for Christians and Moslems and Jews as for Buddhists. Both are built on the naturalistic observations of humans and on careful introspection by their founders. I think that as you read about constructive living you will be thinking that it isn't so very mystical and Oriental but rather practical and human and, well, realistic.

## MORITA THERAPY

Let us begin our consideration of Morita's ideas with the topic of feelings. Feelings are an important part of human life. There are feelings we like (feelings like confidence and love and happiness and satisfaction) and feelings we don't like (like loneliness and depression and fear and timidity). It isn't surprising that we try to generate some feelings and eliminate others. The problem with feelings, however, is that we cannot control them directly by our will. We cannot sit down and concentrate and make our shyness go away or make ourselves stop feeling lonely on a Saturday night or make ourselves fall in love or out of love with someone. It just cannot be done. We cannot make ourselves stop feeling nervous before an exam or anxious before asking someone out on a date or tense before a job interview. Feelings are natural consequences of who we are and the situations we are in, just like clouds are natural consequences of temperatures and pressures and humidity and so forth. Feelings are natural and, naturally, they are just as uncontrollable as the weather.

DAVID K. REYNOLDS

Now, no one tries to fight with rain or fog. You never see anyone going outside waving a sword or a karate blow at rain clouds. And no ordinary humans try by their will to make fog go away. No one ignores the weather, but we have all learned to dim our headlights in the fog, stay inside during hurricanes, and so forth. And we do what we can reasonably do while waiting for bad weather to pass.

Feelings are just like that. The best way to handle unpleasant feelings is to recognize them (don't try to ignore them or pretend they aren't there), to accept them (you can't control them directly, why try to fight something you can't defeat anyway?), and to go on about doing what you need to do. Rain or fog may not stop you from going to school or to work, but you will take the weather into consideration while driving. In the same way, anxiety need not stop you from studying or asking for a raise in pay, though you'll take it into consideration while selecting a place and time to study or a proper moment to approach your boss. And in time, unpleasant feelings pass, just like snowstorms. Grief, for example, never sustains its intensity forever. It fades little by little over time unless something comes along to restimulate it again, then it fades again. Just like changeable weather.

As you can see, I'm making a clear distinction between feelings and behavior. Feelings are natural phenomena, uncontrollable directly by our will; they come and go like weather. Behavior (preparing for an interview, for example, or dealing with a difficult client) is controllable. We can choose to dress properly for an interview (behavior) even though we cannot choose to get rid of our anxiety (feeling) about it. We can ask someone out on a date (behavior) while feeling shy. We can total up the check at a restaurant (behavior) even though we cannot choose to avoid our unpleasant feelings about making others wait while we do so. Just as we can decide to go on a picnic even though the day is windy. This distinction between directly controllable behavior and directly uncontrollable feelings is a key feature of Moritist thought.

If we have no direct control over something, we cannot

be held responsible for it. Who is responsible for an earthquake? We aren't responsible for having angry, spiteful, depressed, sexy, grumpy, greedy, or any other kind of feelings. Again, feelings are natural. On the other hand, we are responsible for what we do, our behavior, no matter what we are feeling. Behavior (except for a few areas, like stuttering and sexual impotence and trembling) is controllable by our will, so we are responsible for that aspect of our lives all the time. To be sure, we find it convenient to try to escape from our responsibility for our actions by blaming our feelings. "I was so angry I couldn't help hitting him"; "I was too distraught to thank her"; "I feel the need for drugs is so strong that I steal to get them." But these feeling-based excuses don't hold water. Similarly, blaming parents or society or spouses or children for our destructive behavior is to seek to avoid responsibility for what is rightfully our own responsibility no matter what past experiences we may have suffered through.

One of the interesting things about humans is that what we do (our behavior) often influences how we feel. We never have direct control over our natural feelings, but sometimes we can affect our affect by our actions. If you don't feel like going on a job interview one morning, it seems to me that it is a waste of time to try to make yourself want to do so. I think it is natural to feel some hesitation about laying your ego on the line for someone else to decide whether you are worthy of hiring or not. There is no need to make yourself enjoy job interviews. The solution? Simply to get out of bed, get dressed for the interview, and go. Sometimes, in the dressing and reading over your résumé and driving over to the appointment a sort of excitement and interest in what will happen arises. Sometimes it doesn't. In either case, the interview gets done. Doing a few job interviews well, succeeding at them, having jobs offered to you as a result, may make job hunting even pleasurable. But lying in bed, putting off getting up, and failing to show up for the job interview never gives you a chance to succeed, never gives you a chance to feel anything but uncomfortable about job interviews. The more we allow feelings to govern our lives, the more they spread to govern even larger areas of life.

So we can use our behavior to give ourselves the chance to succeed at accomplishing our goals. And that success often produces confidence and other satisfying feelings.

Pleasant feelings fade over time just as unpleasant ones do, unless something happens to restimulate those feelings. Romantic love fades in a lot of marriages. Respect for individuals and school spirit and patriotic feelings toward one's country can be expected to fade unless restimulated somehow. That's what dates and rallies and national anthems are about. In the doing of these things, certain feelings are likely to be stimulated or restimulated. If you want to keep love in your relationship, you must keep doing kindness for your partner. As you behave in thoughtful, loving ways, you are increasing the chances of sustaining feelings of love for him or her. Romance in a marriage is sustained by gifts and candle-lit dinners and kisses and dressing up for each other and so forth.

But even this focus on influencing feelings indirectly through behavior is a bit unnatural. Sometimes you seem to do everything right, you plan the proper behaviors to generate certain feelings, and the feelings don't turn out as expected. A better strategy for living is to be purpose-focused instead of being feeling-focused. Let the feelings take care of themselves while you go about accomplishing your goals through your behavior. As the emphasis in your life turns more and more toward using controllable behavior to achieve your goals, life steadies down and becomes more satisfying. I am not talking here of the tunnel-vision workaholic who focuses only on business and economic success. Purposes and goals are various. But on the whole, being purpose-oriented will pay off more than being feeling-oriented, simply because the latter isn't a game you can win with any consistency. You can't make good feelings last and last; you can't make bad feelings go away at will. (Technically, it isn't proper to use words like *good* and *bad* when referring to feelings; like seasons, they have no moral qualities.)

If feelings are natural phenomena, doesn't it seem strange to you that there are psychotherapies that try to make fears or guilt or depression go away? There are psychotherapies and self-growth methods that aim at producing happiness and confidence and good feelings about yourself all the time. I cannot see how such therapies can deliver on their promises. No one is happy or confident or feeling good about anything all the time. Feelings keep changing, like the sky keeps changing. A more suitable goal for therapy, or for human life in general, seems to be to notice and accept these changes in feelings while keeping steadily on about doing the things that will get us where we want to go. Like water does.

Morita therapy holds that all humans are oversensitive to their own faults and limits to some degree. Especially when we are ill or under stress, we may become fixated on some mental or physical disturbance. We blow out of proportion the ringing in our ears or our stiff shoulder or our fear of flying or our discomfort about eating in restaurants or whatever. The proper course to alleviate these problem areas is not to ignore them or to fight them but to accept them while getting on about proper, constructive behavior. In other words, whatever is troubling us, it is important to accept the troubled feelings and get on about living. Of course, if there is something practical and concrete we can do to alleviate the cause of the problem (such as seeing a physician to rule out organic illness), that is included in the category of proper, constructive behavior.

In general, the stronger we desire something, the more we want to succeed, the greater our anxiety about failure. Our worries and fears are reminders of the strength of our positive desires. They are also reminders of our needs to use caution, prepare materials to avoid the embarrassment of lack of preparation, work hard, practice perfecting our skills, develop our ability to persist and endure, attack the environmental circumstances that caused them, and so forth. Our anxieties are indispensable for us in spite of the discomfort accompanying them. To try to do away with them would be foolish. Morita therapy is not really a psychotherapeutic method for getting rid of "symptoms." It is more an educational method for outgrowing our self-imposed limitations. Through Moritist methods we learn to accept the naturalness of ourselves.

In their advanced stages, Morita students accept themselves as part of the natural situation in which they are embedded. I do not refer to some passive conformity but to a dynamic recognition that we exist as situationally embedded aspects of reality. We take on our identities from the circumstances in which we find ourselves. We are rather like the cursor markers on the computer screen of reality. The loss of self-centeredness, in more than one sense of the word, is an ultimate goal for some students of this method. However, relief from the obsessive pressure of phobias, anxieties, and psychosomatic difficulties is sufficient for many students.

Currently, there are more than five thousand members of the Seikatsu no Hakkenkai Moritist organization in Japan. There are more than fifty practitioners of Morita therapy in the United States, Canada, West Germany, and the People's Republic of China. A growing literature exists in English, with seven books in print and several more in press and numerous articles and book chapters on the subject. Morita's collected works fill seven thick volumes. From this, rich source-material adaptations are made to fit the needs of modern Japanese and non-Japanese students. Morita therapy is growing inside and outside Japan as never before.

What we have considered here so far has come from the thought of the Japanese psychiatrist Morita Shoma (or Morita Masatake, as he preferred to call himself). Now, let's turn briefly to the contribution to constructive living made by the lay priest Yoshimoto Ishin and his Naikan.

NAIKAN

One of the factors that seems to influence how we feel is our attitude toward the world. If we are constantly concerned with getting our share, with making sure we aren't left out, if we are extremely self-focused and self-conscious, then we are likely to have a lot of miserable feelings. The world just never seems to send us green lights and lottery prizes and kind words when we want them. And we want them nearly all the time.

Have you ever stopped to think about how much of you is truly yours? Your name was given to you by your parents. So was your body. The words you use were taught to you by parents and peers and teachers. Your body has grown and is sustained by food that people you don't even know produced and processed for you. The clothes you wear were created and sewn by others, bought with money given to you by someone else. Even the ideas you have seem to bubble to the surface of your mind, coming out of nowhere and passing along to be replaced by other thoughts from nowhere. There's nothing that is truly yours; it is all borrowed. Of course, it is the same for all of us.

You may say, of course, that you bought your clothes with your own money. But who gave you the money? Who taught you to do the work you do that earned the money? Who hired you? Who gave you the basic educational skills to learn the trade you ply? The point is that when we trace back our achievements far enough, we see the fruits of others' efforts in our behalf, inevitably. We have done nothing on our own.

Strange, then, that we should have the notion that we are self-made. We believe that we got where we are by our own efforts. With just a little bit of reflection we can see that such notions of having come this far on our own are laughable. Deeper reflection allows us to see in even greater detail how we have been, and continue to be, supported on all sides in all sorts of ways by people and things and energies (such as electricity and the sun's heat and light).

One result of sorting out the specific, concrete ways in which the world supports us (just as you are supporting me now by loaning me your eyes to read this chapter) is a feeling of gratitude. I don't deserve all this help from you and this paper and the electricity that powers this word processor (and the people who worked to generate this electricity) and the editor and publisher of

DAVID K. REYNOLDS

this book and the manufacturers of this printer's ink, book design-ers, and the people who taught me these lifeways, and so forth. But through Naikan, we can come to notice and appreciate the surrounding nurturance from the world and to offer words of thanks. Before I underwent a week of Naikan training in Japan, I thought all this was my due. I took it for granted, and drift back into that attitude sometimes still. But whether I recognize it or not, whether I accept it or not, whether I feel gratitude or not, whether I try to return the favors or not, reality keeps on being what it is. It keeps on giving to me, not in some abstract sense, but concretely, through Jim and Frank and Lynn and this keyboard and so forth·

So the natural response to realizing what is really going on is the desire to repay, and a sort of guilt when we see that we haven't been doing much repaying right along. Starting with our parents, our attitude shifts from how little we have received from them and how much more they owe us to one of how much we have received from them and how important it is to start working on giving back something to them. I'm not suggesting that all par-ents are perfect and that they have done a perfect job in raising us. But I am asserting that there were some adults in our lives who fed and clothed us and nurtured us when we were small. They did it whether they were in the mood or not, over and over again, whether we felt appreciative or showed them gratitude or not—or we wouldn't have survived to be here today.

The gratitude and desire to repay apply to the people in your life today, as well, and to objects in your world. What have you done for your shoes lately, for your car, for electricity, for your toothbrush and stereo set? If you take a moment to consider what they have done for you, it seems not quite so odd to think of what you might do for them in return.

I've never met a suffering neurotic person who was filled with gratitude. Isn't that something? Gratitude and neurotic suffering seem to be antagonistic. If there is anything characteristic of neu-rosis it is a self-centeredness. Gratitude, on the other hand, is other-centered. It carries with it the desire to serve others in repayment, even if it causes some inconvenience to oneself.

The most joyful people I have known have all been people who gave themselves away to others. The most miserable people I have known have all been concerned with looking out for themselves. Check with your own experience, look around. Despite commercials to the contrary, looking out for number one is a sure path to torment.

### THE PRACTICE OF CONSTRUCTIVE LIVING

How does one go about doing Morita therapy and Naikan? Both therapies have what might be called inpatient and outpatient styles. The inpatient styles are only occasionally practiced in countries other than Japan. The outpatient styles have been modified somewhat for Westerners. Interestingly, however, the modified outpatient styles for Westerners have been reintroduced to Japan, where they strongly influence the practice of these therapies there.

### *Inpatient Morita Therapy*

Inpatient Morita therapy begins with a week of isolated bed rest. Within the Moritist hospital, the patient is not permitted to read or write or converse or smoke or engage in any distraction other than eating three meals a day and taking care of other natural body functions. There is no escape from the waves of doubt, boredom, anxiety, regret, and the like that pass through the mind (more accurately, they *are* the mind in that setting). Past failures are reviewed mentally, along with future potential troubles. Despite the suffering, time passes and the patient survives. Feelings and thoughts well up and fade. The patient learns some measure of acceptance of these mental phenomena. And the patient becomes bored. It is unnatural to lie in retreat from the world when we are physically capable of constructive activity. The desire to move about emerges.

Subsequent stages of inpatient Morita therapy offer the patient scaled tasks, including weeding the garden, writing a journal of activities, participating in group sports, household chores, errands off the hospital grounds and, finally, return to everyday life outside the hospital. Constructive activity provides a distraction from rumination about neurotic misery. In time, reality's tasks are carried out simply because they need to be done whether the symptoms are present or not. In fact, the subjective experience of symptoms declines over time; but that decline is merely a pleasant byproduct of being able to do what needs doing while suffering or not.

The entire period of hospitalization varies considerably from place to place and patient to patient. Perhaps two or three months is the mean these days, although Morita himself began inpatient treatment in the 1920s with a period of about one month.

### Outpatient Morita Therapy

Outpatient Morita therapy involves teaching the student the principles of living (rather as they have been described here) and inviting the student to compare these concepts with his or her own experience. Whether the principles are fully understood or not, assignments are made to give the student increasing experiential knowledge about the lifeway. For example, the student may be advised to get up at a particular time whether feeling like it or not, make the bed, prepare breakfast and eat it regardless of anxieties or dreadful anticipation of what might happen during the day. The student may be asked to observe and report on detailed behaviors, such as which foot touched the floor first when arising from bed, what was done with the toothpaste cap while brushing the teeth, and so forth. The focus is on attending to the activities rather than on complaints about mental anguish.

Reading assignments are given. Other techniques include keeping a Morita journal separating behaviors and feelings, discussion of fables illustrating psychological truths, and homework tasks of various sorts. Moritist maxims help the client keep the life principles in mind throughout the day. (More detailed descriptions of assignments and other techniques are to be found in Reynolds, 1984, 1986, 1987, and Ishiyama, 1987.)

### Inpatient Naikan Therapy

Inpatient Naikan therapy involves a week of intensive reflection on the three themes of 1) what was received from some person; 2) what was done in return for that person; and 3) what troubles and worries were caused that person. The Naikan client spends each day from early morning until night in isolated reflection on these themes. At first, the mother or mother surrogate is the object of reflection. What did my mother do for me during the first three years of grammar school? What did I do in return for her? What troubles did I cause her? After a period of time, perhaps an hour or two, the therapist comes to listen to the Naikan client's accounting of what was recalled. The therapist listens gratefully, without comment or interpretation. Then, during the next period of Naikan meditation, the same three themes will be considered regarding the mother during the client's fourth- through sixth-grade years. Again, the therapist comes to listen. The pattern progresses in approximately three year intervals up to the present or until the mother died. Then the client begins again with the grammar-school period, working on the recollections of the father in the same sequence. Working from the past up to the present, the client works on other significant persons in his or her life.

The method is simple, but it has a very powerful emotional impact on the clients. In effect, they measure themselves by their own standards of reciprocity and find themselves wanting. There is no escape into the deflection that they are being tested by someone else's standards (some formal religious code, for example). Guilt and gratitude and a sense of having been loved in spite of one's failings and the desire to try to repay others are common results of inpatient Naikan therapy.

After the week is over, clients are encouraged to continue Naikan during shorter periods each day. Each morning the client is to continue reflections about others in the past just as during the hospital period. In the evening the client is advised to reflect about that day—what was received from others during the day, what was returned to them, and what troubles the client caused others during the day.

## Outpatient Naikan Therapy

Outpatient Naikan therapy may take the form of daily Naikan reflection as described immediately above. The student may be asked to keep a journal of Naikan recollections and to bring the journal to the weekly outpatient sessions. Related assignments include saying thank you a minimum of ten times each day, particularly to a person with whom the student is currently on bad terms. Quarreling spouses are likely to receive assignments to bring gifts to each other and to perform services for each other in secret. To be sure, there is resistance to such assignments. The students may complain that they feel no gratitude toward their spouse and so cannot say thank you. They may hold that the spouse doesn't deserve their words of gratitude, gifts, and services. At such times they are given the Moritist reminder of the difference between feelings (such as gratitude), which are uncontrollable and for which they have no responsibility, and behaviors (such as thanking and giving gifts), which remain in their control.

Another outpatient Naikan therapy assignment is to ask the student to clean out a drawer. The items are removed from the drawer and the drawer cleaned. Then the items are returned to the drawer one by one. As each item is returned, it is thanked for some specific service it performed for the student. We are served not only by people but also by the energies and objects in our world. Conservation of the resources in our world becomes a natural consequence of the grateful recognition of the services they perform for us.

### COMMON FEATURES

The outpatient forms of both Morita and Naikan therapy are directive and follow an education model rather than a medical model of dealing with human suffering. Understanding the principles of the lifeway of constructive living is an important element in achieving some release from unnecessary misery. The students' efforts to change their behavior are seen to be important in constructive living.

Both elements of constructive living are concerned with reality. Whether you believe it or not, accept it or not, like it or not, reality is "as it is."

> Why fret away your life?
> See the willow tree by the river;
> There it is, watching the water flow by.*

Pay attention to what reality brings you, both Morita's therapy and Yoshimoto's Naikan advise. Check out reality directly. Don't simply accept what I or anyone else tells you about the way things are. See for yourself. Your understanding of psychology must not be founded solely on what you read in some textbooks or heard in lectures. It must be experiential or it will not be of maximum usefulness to you.

Both elements of constructive living have an action emphasis. It isn't enough to accept feelings, it isn't enough to feel gratitude; it is important to *do* something constructive, purposeful. We owe the world for our existence. We will never find life satisfaction without making efforts to repay that debt. Being mature and psychologically healthy doesn't mean feeling good all the time. Maturity means acting responsibly, positively, whether we feel good or not, grateful or not.

Finally, both elements of constructive living look pragmatically at what is possible and what is impossible. Morita therapy advises that we cannot change our feelings directly by our will, that we cannot control other people directly, that we cannot control completely the outcome of our efforts. We do our best to influence these uncontrollable aspects of our lives, but we must accept what reality actually brings us. Naikan recognizes that we cannot directly change what happened in our past. We can influence our way of looking at the past, our attitude toward the past. And we

*Shibayama, 1970, p. 261.

DAVID  K.  REYNOLDS

can work to create a new past by our actions in the present. But as events flow into the past, they are fixed forever. We must accept them as reality. Being clear about what is possible and what is impossible in life helps us avoid wasting attention and energy; we become wiser about the proper directions in which to invest our efforts.

> Not knowing how close the Truth is to them,
> Beings seek for it afar—what a pity!
> It is like those who being in water
> Cry out for water, feeling thirst.*

*Shibayama, 1970, p. 93

## No Magic

How many people are searching for some magical salvation! How disappointed they must eventually become! The sort of salvation they seek would reduce them to the status of children playing happily in a protected paradise free of troubles and unpleasant feelings. Such a paradise exists only in their imagination.

There is nothing magical that will save them from life's natural misery. No prayer, no insight, no mantra, no positive thinking, no meditation, no medical technique, no chemical, no psychological formula will simplify and solve life's difficulties and barriers. It's tough, but that's the way life is.

Nearly anyone can make a living by offering some miraculous freedom from human suffering, some endless joy, some direct control over emotions. Nearly anyone can find desperate followers to believe the most absurd claims and promises. But people with their eyes on reality are beginning to see the foolishness and emptiness of miracle cures for living. We would like to believe in simple magic, but we have experienced and observed that it doesn't work consistently or predictably if at all.

It is time to grow up. Only effortful, purposefully directed action gives us a chance to accomplish what we aim for in life. We must endure some pain, self-doubts, worry, and disappointment as part of the whole package of being human. There is no shopping list from which we can choose the items of our existence, in consumer fashion.

Of course, there is some suffering that can be realistically and sensibly avoided. We don't go for a solitary stroll in certain parts of big cities late at night, for example. But to hold out for anxiety-free living is childish. To reach for risk-free, failure-free, worry-free, stress-free, joy-all-the-time living is pitifully impractical. Who lives that kind of life? I haven't met a person who is free of suffering. Have you?

So it is time we got on about doing what is possible in life. It is time we accepted the limits and possibilities life offers us and pressed toward fulfilling our genuine potential. Therein lies reality-based satisfaction.

## What Constructive Living Won't Do for You

Constructive living won't give you constant joy, peace, or self-confidence.

Constructive living won't make you rich, successful, or famous.

Constructive living won't make you forget about him or her, about that blunder, your loss, the chance you missed, the punishment you didn't deserve.

Constructive living won't get rid of your worries, anxiety, fears.

Constructive living won't necessarily make you more loving, more grateful, more giving.

Constructive living won't necessarily improve your life, your character, your future.

Constructive living won't necessarily turn you into a better person, a deeper person, a wiser person, a more settled person.

Sounds useless, doesn't it? All those things you would like to become, and constructive living won't help you attain those ideals.

Of course, no other method will turn you into your ideal either. Your own efforts may bring about some of these desired changes, but frankly speaking, constructive living doesn't have much to offer people who will be satisfied only when they attain the states of perfection listed above.

　　　　　　　　　　　　**DAVID K. REYNOLDS**

What does constructive living have to offer? With a lot of purposeful, dedicated effort you can become *you*. But you are already you; you couldn't be anyone else. Constructive living can help you learn to accept the natural you—the you with your desires to succeed and your fears of failing; the you with your search for good health and your fears of illness and dying; the you with your wishes for perfection and your disappointment with limitations; the you who (sometimes) feels foolish, embarrassed, lacking in confidence, frightened, angry, worried, vulnerable, timid, but also (at times) caring, grateful, hopeful, giving, loving, accepting. Constructive living helps you recognize yourself as you really are, accept the whole mixed bag of you, and get on about living. Constructive living is a way to become nothing special. Don't you get tired of trying to be extraordinary, superior, wonderfully enlightened? Wouldn't it be a relief just to be you, nothing-special you, but putting-out-your-best you?

What happens to you after you catch on (and keep catching on) to the reality of yourself is not nearly as important as simply accepting yourself as you are. You may become successful and famous or not; you may deepen your wisdom and character or not; you may find more peace of mind or not. Whatever comes your way, you will be able to look it in the eye and do what you need to do about it.

That's all constructive living has to offer. Just all that really matters. As Morita put it, "The view from the high mountain is worth the climb."

*Only Context*

There is only context.

In an issue of *Science 85* magazine I read a couple of short articles that emphasized the importance of knowing the natural context in which an event occurs. In one study it was found that the trout in Prickly Pear Creek in Montana are thriving in water with mineral-pollution levels even ten times above those set as acceptable by EPA standards. The standards were set based on experiments with pollution levels and fish in laboratories. It turns out that in some natural conditions, fish are able to build tolerances that allow them to survive in settings that are lethal to fish suddenly introduced to the very same levels in the laboratory.

The lab conditions oversimplified the model that was expected to apply to natural conditions. The conclusions of the studies couldn't be extended beyond the lab setting in any simple fashion.

In the same magazine was an article about a flying cricket with a neuron that fires when exposed to ultrasound in the range that bats ordinarily emit. The neuron connects to motor nerves that steer the cricket away from the sound, *but only when the cricket is flying.* When the cricket is mating or grooming or on the ground, the escape behavior is not triggered. You could pin a cricket down in the lab and monitor the firing of its neurons and never come across the connection between flying and ultrasound and escape

　　　　　　　　　　　　　　　**DAVID K. REYNOLDS**

behavior. Without some notion of context the findings would be limited trivia.

It's not a big step from "circumstances cause me to act in certain ways" to "circumstances are me." Some people will be frightened by this ephemeral possibility of the self. They want an identity more solid than what is rooted in the fragile base of ever-shifting circumstances. Those people want a fictional self. I am not talking about a philosophical possibility. I am talking about reality. To look closely is to see it. Some don't know how to look; some are afraid to look. The truth is that the only sounds "I" hear are sounds other than the "me" that is listening; the only sights "I" see are sights other than the "me" that is seeing. The only world that "I" know is the world of "my" circumstances, the thoughts and sensations and feelings that bubble into awareness from "outside." No matter how hard I look or listen, I cannot see or hear this mind of mine. It seems to be nothing more than a field or screen on which phenomena move about. Perhaps it is nothing more than the phenomena it reflects. Perhaps it is reflections.

# *Vitamins and Fine-tuning*

## VITAMINS

Constructive living is in some ways like vitamins. I don't want to push the analogy too far, but let's take a look at some of the parallels. Vitamins are useful for healthy people as well as sick ones. The more one pushes oneself, the more they are needed. People who exercise a lot, for example, require more vitamins. In troubled, stressful times, too, our bodies demand more vitamins. Vitamins are found in our everyday meals. Finally, vitamins contribute to our bodies' resistance to the misfortune of illness. They are preventative and constructive, not surgical in nature.

Constructive living, too, is useful for people who would be considered quite mentally fit, even superior. People who would be labeled neurotic can also benefit from this lifeway.

Constructive-living principles are useful in our lives at all times, but we particularly appreciate them when we are pushing ahead to achieve our goals, when we are in stressful situations, when life demands much from us.

Constructive living becomes part of our everyday life. It is as common as taking a meal or a nap. It constitutes our daily living.

Constructive living is not a medicine. It doesn't aim to cure anything. It aims, rather, at building character. Character is built

**DAVID K. REYNOLDS**

on habits; habits are built on each moment's behavior. Whatever reality sends our way we are better prepared to handle through constructive living. In some ways constructive living resembles a vitamin for living, vitamin L.

## FINE-TUNING

When we begin the path of constructive living, there are usually major obvious changes in our life style. Life tends to become more simplified and more organized. Priorities change. We become more productive. We pay more attention to the details of living. But even after we have roughed out the sculpture of our constructive lives, there is still attention and energy and need for more detailed work. I call such work fine-tuning.

One area of fine-tuning occurs in discovering what needs to be done. We have principles about observing what reality brings, admonitions about looking to this moment's needs more often than being caught up in grand and distant goal-dreaming, and techniques like writing our own obituaries, epitaphs, and eulogies, as you may know from reading my earlier books. But even with the focus on this moment, we humans seem to need a general direction in which to move. Modern cultures and modern times offer a variety of directions unlike those narrow choices provided in Morita's era. Objectivity, humanism, and Naikan-like values seem to underlie or complement the Morita lifeway. Many students want long-term direction spelled out for them. I struggle with the desire to meet their stated needs and the resistance to add *my* values to the technique. Or are the values not mine, but an integral part of the method? Now thinking, thinking, thinking.

I ask those who attend my workshops to introduce themselves and tell the group why they came to the workshop. From the beginning we talk about goals, purposes. The purposes I hear from the individuals in the group modify my purposes and methods in teaching. And my teaching may affect the purposes my students have for attending the workshop.

But in the final analysis we discover meaning in life not by figuring it out beforehand, not by sitting and talking about it. We discover life meaning by acting in life, by doing. In the doing we create purposes as we go along. Purposeless people are in real trouble. They are paralyzed people. We construct our talk about our life goals and life meaning from the countless acts of moment-by-moment living. Most often we see the pattern of a segment of our lives *after* we have lived it.

# *Morita Therapy as a Constructive Life Style*

(In slightly revised form, this essay was presented on November 3, 1984, in Tokyo as a lecture in Japanese to a meeting of Seikatsu no Hakkenkai [the Discovery of Life Organization], the largest Moritist organization in the world.)

Let us consider expansion, broadening, outgrowing old definitions and old limits. There are two levels worthy of our thinking here—on the personal level, I shall refer to the ways in which we each learn to overcome the limits we place on ourselves. Morita therapy has helped many of us recognize the unrealistic limits that clutter our lives and do something about them. On another level, we can reflect upon the ways we can overcome the limits that have been placed on Morita's ideas as a system. I intend to suggest ways in which we can make Morita therapy more accessible and helpful to many more people than just those labeled *shinkeishitsu,* or "neurotically oversensitive."

## OUTGROWING OUR OLD SELVES

The way we discover ourselves, the way we create our identity, is to look back on our past and see what kind of people we were. If we did timid things we see ourselves as timid; if we did adventurous things we see ourselves as adventurous. The way to change the way we see ourselves is to change our past. Right now we are in the process of creating a new past. What we do now will become our past when we look back on our actions tomorrow. We change who we are by changing what we do.

In stories from my earlier writings (e.g., "The Doll Carriage," "Hiding Under the Sofa," and "One Step Forward, Two Steps Back") were characters who created new identities for themselves through their behavior in the present. It was easy to see the limits these people placed on their own lives seeking a return to childhood, security, and certainty. Reality doesn't allow us the safety, security, and certainty of true childhood after we have become adults. We must risk in order to accomplish, in order to succeed, in order to grow.

### OUTGROWING THE THERAPY LABEL

Therapies, too, have a kind of identity created through their past history.

There is a history of constructive living just as there is a history for each one of us. The Morita-therapy element of constructive living began as a treatment form for neurotic oversensitivity. It was used by physicians to treat this narrow range of neurotic problems in Japan. But over the years it has grown to be used on a wider range of human problems in a number of countries. And it is practiced not only by physicians but by psychologists, social workers, teachers, ministers, managers, and others. At one time Morita therapy was only practiced in the home of Morita; now it is taught in outpatient clinics and in correspondence courses and in study groups and in retreat settings and in colleges in America and in public lectures. You can see that constructive living has grown and broadened. I think that constructive living is in a stage of adolescence. Just like an adolescent, it is in search of its adult identity.

Some people would like to see constructive living remain

DAVID K. REYNOLDS

within the narrow domain of elite physicians. They would like to see it return to its childhood, like the girl in the doll-carriage story. But the hospitals for Morita therapy are few in Japan and nonexistent elsewhere. And the number of young physicians who are truly interested in doing only Morita therapy are few also. There is no future for constructive living as a narrow medical practice. It is not economical as medical treatment for patients or for physicians, either.

But there is a way for constructive-living ideas to outgrow their historical limitations. There is a way for constructive living to achieve adulthood. There are risks involved, but the potential rewards are great. Let me paint a word picture for you of this constructive-living movement twenty-five years from now.

I predict that the word *therapy* will no longer be used for constructive living. We will be talking about the constructive life-style or living fully or something of that sort. Constructive-living ideas are practical and useful to everyone, not just to sensitive neurotics. So they will be applied more broadly outside the medical setting. Morita called his method reeducation. The life education aspects of his method will be emphasized within twenty-five years. Rather than *doctor* and *patient,* we will be using words like *teacher* or *guide* and *student.*

Physicians will still be consulted to help with diagnosis and treatment of the few people with chemical disorders of the brain like schizophrenia and manic depression, but physicians won't do much of the teaching of this lifeway. They will be too busy with genuine medical problems. Absolute isolated bed rest (the above-mentioned technique of inpatient Morita therapy) won't be practiced in hospitals but in retreats like Ashigara Ryo, the Seikatsu no Hakkenkai organization's mountain retreat facility.

Around the world, constructive living organizations will offer a wide variety of activities for members. Already there are Moritist groups in Japan for poetry, baking, English conversation, hiking, flower arrangement, reading, sports, social activities, and so forth. The purpose of these groups is not only to develop particular skills, but also to bring together people with similar interests and similar problems in their lives so they can learn from one another. Our constructive lifeway must be learned by everyday action as well as by listening and reading. I expect new activities like travel groups to various parts of the world, shopping expeditions, home-repair classes, dance clubs, writing workshops, and bazaars will emerge. I wouldn't be surprised if twenty-five years from now there were at least one constructive-living publishing company, constructive-living supermarkets, constructive-living hotels and inns.

This expansion of constructive-living productions won't be merely a commercial venture. It will be a demonstration that the constructive lifeway is applicable to all of life—not only interpersonal relationships and the task at hand, but to business and to leisure and to all of self-development and constructive exploration. Sensitive people will be the leaders of this movement for two reasons: 1) they benefit most from turning their attention from inner suffering to constructive activity so they recognize the value of these life principles; and 2) sensitive people are persistent and self-sacrificing when they find a purposeful way to live. Nevertheless, the membership of constructive-living organizations will expand to include people who have relatively few sensitive moments (everyone has some sensitive qualities, Morita pointed out). Whether a person is sensitive or not, he or she can perceive the positive and meaningful nature of these suggestions for living.

Naikan has become an important element in constructive living, as well. More and more, Naikan-like thinking and assignments can be seen in Morita-therapy practice in Japan. Attention to the ways we are supported by the world results in gratitude and a desire to repay others. Neurotically suffering people become more aware of the effects of their self-centeredness on others. They make greater efforts to live positively in order to relieve the burden on their loved ones, while improving their own lives.

This broadened approach to constructive living using Morita's

DAVID K. REYNOLDS

ideas and Yoshimoto's Naikan is the path we are following in the United States. Recently, this trend can be seen in Japan, too. There will come a time when Morita's and Yoshimoto's ideas will help build better understanding and better relations between our countries across the Pacific.

# Searching for the Source

By now you are familiar with the notion that feelings are natural aspects of reality. If we take the trouble to search, we can find a natural, understandable source for any feeling. One source of any anxious feeling, for example, is a strong desire. Anxiety about failing comes from a strong desire to succeed. Anxiety about meeting people comes from a strong desire to be liked and respected. The stronger the positive desire, the greater is the anxiety associated with it. Dr. Takehisa Kora, a Morita therapist in Tokyo, has written on this subject in great detail. In the United States, we sometimes ask our students to look for the positive desire underlying their specific fears and worries. When they discover the underlying constructive desires, they are better able to accept the naturalness of the anxieties, too.

But the search for the deep, hidden origins of our unpleasant feelings isn't always so important. Whether we discover the source or not, all feelings are the natural result of our life situations. Recognize it or not, accept it or not, emotions are no more than another natural aspect of our life reality. We may survey our feelings, however, to discern whether they are pointing toward some necessary action.

The attitude of acceptance of feelings is much more important than the search for their deep origins. Acceptance puts emotions

DAVID K. REYNOLDS

in proper perspective. They occur, we recognize them, and we go on about doing what it is necessary to do in our lives. In fact, the search for the deep sources of our feelings can falsely validate an importance they need not carry in our lives. The search can distract us from the constructive behaviors that lie right before our eyes. Haven't you met people who are so caught up in discovering the hidden sources of their distressing feelings that their lives appear to be at a standstill? They are so involved in introspection that their houses aren't clean and their offices are cluttered with work undone.

Creative artists, however, may find it useful to explore their feelings in detail in order to discover novelties worth expressing in their work. Lay people, too, may wish to explore their feelings for the sheer fascination of the intricacy to be found there, the connections with the rest of reality. Nevertheless, such a hobby must be kept in perspective and balanced with constructive, purposeful action. Failure to do so will inevitably lead to aimless wandering in the labyrinths of the mind, a selfish and ultimately unsatisfying preoccupation.

For most of us, it is sufficient to accept the emotions that surface, check to see whether they suggest some necessary action (pain, for example, may tell us to get our hands off the hot stove), act appropriately to the circumstances, and get on about noticing and responding to other aspects of reality.

## Helping Out

One morning Joshu was walking in front of the Zen Hall, treading on the deep-drifted snow. He accidentally lost his footing and fell in the snow. He cried out loudly, "Help me out! Help me out!" A monk heard him crying, came running, raising clouds, and instead of helping the Master out of the snow, "threw himself in the snow too." That is, the monk laid himself down in the snow like the Master. Joshu, who could very well have given the monk a blow of his stick, quite calmly returned to his room.

Now, did this monk help the old teacher out or not?*

Sometimes there is nothing we can do to take away the difficulty that is troubling someone we care about. He may be dying or suffering because someone close to him has died. She may have put herself in trouble or danger, a situation that we cannot salvage for her. No matter how strong our desire to help, we may be unable to change the distressing circumstances.

At such times we may decide to throw ourselves into the snow alongside our friend. We may choose to share some of the misery and physical discomfort, to talk about the loss, to empathize, to

*Shibayama, 1970, p. 226.

DAVID K. REYNOLDS

donate our time and our existence in order to be with our friend as he grieves. Our efforts may not solve the problem; they may not even relieve much of our friend's pain. But it is a fine human gesture to dive into the snow anyway. It may be the best we can do. For her. For us. For Us.

Contrast the effort of diving into the snow with the indifference described by Soseki:

> Daisuke has yet to meet the individual who, as he stood groaning beneath the oppression of Occidental civilization in the seething arena of the struggle for survival, was still able to shed genuine tears for another.*

Soseki was a perceptive critic of the dangers that accompanied the benefits of Western civilization as Japan adopted Western ways around the turn of this century. Competition in the economic sphere can spill over into a self-centered indifference to others' dilemmas in other areas of life. Especially in this modern era of an unseemly faith in economic measures of importance, we must beware the danger of losing compassion. To dive into the snow is "doing compassion."

Some of the places in the modern world where I have seen compassion done are terminal-care units in hospitals. I have spent time with dying people and those who care for them in Japan and in the United States. There seems to be a kind of humanization of the participants in some of those settings. I'd like to consider some of the qualities that compose this humanization.

Let's begin with a small but not unimportant matter. Gifts are given frequently. The gifts are usually inexpensive, personal, and sometimes handmade. Among nurses, aides, patients, families, and doctors, and within some of these groups, small gifts are tokens of human worth—exchanged appreciation, treasured mementos, spots of bright color in pastel medical surroundings.

People listen more and better in these settings. They show spe-

*Soseki, 1978, p. 102.

cial consideration for others. They give time above that required by their shifts.

People use time well, purposefully. It may appear that they are merely sitting and chatting, but they have given thought to the value of such activities.

Some social conventions are waived or postponed. In conversations, people get down to business more quickly. People speak more openly and straightforwardly about their desires, frustrations, worries, joys .

There is a sense of camaraderie among staff, and less of a status gap between patients and staff. People know each others' names.

I am concerned with the needs of caregivers in such settings (medical staff, nursing staff, aides, and officer personnel). They are living/dying just as the patients are, though the slope of their demise may be more gradual. In another sense, each new moment is a birth, and each past moment is a death for them, for all of us.

# An End to Quarreling

In an insightful book, *Being Peace*, written by the Vietnamese monk Thich Nhat Hanh, we can read about the procedures for bringing about reconciliation between quarreling monks in Buddhist monasteries. These methods have been developed over some twenty-five hundred years, representing the experience of humans living closely together for long periods of time. I have adapted some of those principles and combined them with suggestions from Morita and Yoshimoto and an American Moritist, Gregg Krech, to address the needs of modern people who face interpersonal disharmony.

1. *Face the issues:* You may need to get away for a walk, for a period of cooling off, but there must come a time when you face your "other" (the spouse or parent or friend or whomever) in order to deal with the problem. You may wish to settle the matter privately, between the two of you, at first. If that private approach doesn't work out, it is time to call in outside support. Sometimes a friend or relative or professional counselor can mediate the dispute. When the problem remains unresolved, one of a number of further steps is described below.

To call what I am about to suggest a reconciliation party sounds quite strange, but perhaps those words fit the gathering well. The form may be a dinner gathering or a picnic or a prayer meeting or a meditation get-together or any other style of assembly that seems appropriate. The main purpose of the gathering is to bring together a body of people who wish to see the quarreling end. They may be relatives, in-laws, office workers, friends, teammates, national representatives, or any other body of people who suffer from being in contact with the disputants while the fight continues. They want peace.

During the proceedings of the party, the two squabblers must sit facing each other. Symbolically, their facing each other represents their willingness to face the problems that brought about the dispute.

2. *Supportive representation.* It is likely that the quarreling parties have presented their positions to each other more than once. Now is the time for some other person to present each side of the issue. Before the quarreling party, each disputant finds (or is assigned) some person to represent his or her views. The representatives meet with the disputants individually and listen carefully to their arguments, taking notes if necessary. This occasion provides the opportunity for each quarreling member to make his or her case before a third party. At this time it might be helpful to ask each disputant to argue the opponent's position. Is each one clear on the position of the other? Then, before the guests at the gathering, each representative speaks in support of one disputant's view, taking turns.

Hearing one's own position and the position of one's opponent from the lips of another person works to put the matter in a different perspective. But during this period the disputants listen only.

3. *Acknowledgment.* Now it is the turn of the disputants to speak before the gathering. But in this phase they are only allowed to confess their own faults and their own errors and to express the areas in which their opponent deserves gratitude, i.e., areas in which the other has served them, done them favors, given gifts,

and so forth. Of course, this is very difficult. It is not necessary to feel remorseful or grateful. It is only required that each person point out specific instances of ways in which he or she caused trouble for the other and ways in which the other served him or her.

There are many ways to sabotage this part of the reconciliation process. Some people can think of nothing to say, some will speak absurdities or use a sarcastic tone of voice, some will try to hint again of the wrongs done them and the heavier balance of favors they have done to the other. The representatives and other members of the gathering must gently but firmly point out such tendencies, interrupting if necessary until this phase of the process is properly carried out. This is a very important aspect of reconciliation. Be prepared to wait through long pauses until it is fully accomplished.

4. *Superseding purposes.* At this point the antagonists are asked to come up with purposes or goals that are more important than their continued quarreling. They must search for shared purposes and goals that have been disrupted by their quarrel. Again, this phase must not be hurried through with superficial responses. After the disputants have exhausted their examination of this matter, other suggestions may come from the guests at the assembly. It may be helpful to write the shared purposes on a blackboard or large sheet of paper so they can be readily utilized in the next phases of reconciliation.

5. *Specific solutions.* The disputants are invited to present specific alternatives for resolving their quarrel. Further suggestions may come from the other participants.

If a satisfactory resolution can be achieved at this point, the next step can be skipped. The acceptable solution is repeated more than once before the audience. It may be written, if that course is considered useful. The decision must be clear and public.

**6.** *Unanimous decision.* If there remains some substantive decision (e.g., whether to buy the new house, whether to rehire the worker), then it is best for the disputants to agree to abide by the decision of the assembly of guests. Whenever possible, the decision should be based on a unanimous vote taken while the disputants are not present. It takes time and effort to try to arrive at a unanimous decision. Various arguments must be heard, discussed, evaluated. A few recalcitrant members may be difficult to convince; sometimes, their firm convictions sway the thinking of the group back to a unanimous vote in the opposite direction. Again, the investment of time is worth the result.

**6.** *Joint service.* Whatever the result of the final vote, the representatives then call in the disputants and the decision is announced more than once so that everyone is clear about it. Then the two main characters in this drama must shake hands or hug or have some physical contact (feeling like it or not). Finally, the two together must serve those who attended in some way—passing out drinks or offering presents or washing car windshields or any other significant gesture of appreciation and mutual effort in behalf of others.

There may be problems that are not solved by these methods. But I think they are worth a try. They offer more than reconciliation. The determined application of energy toward dealing with the problem has the potential to draw group members together and revalidate their common purposes.

Can you imagine the effect on the United Nations if such a course of reconciliation were adopted? How about those long-standing grudges between relatives, between former friends, between neighbors?

DAVID K. REYNOLDS

# Traveling

I'm doing a lot of traveling these days—away from Los Angeles more than I'm home. Hawaii, New York, Japan, Florida, Pennsylvania, San Francisco, Vancouver—there is growing interest in constructive living in these areas. In Europe and in China, too. I'm discovering that there is much to be learned from a traveling mode of existence.

Travel forces me to look at what is *necessary* to pack. What can I do without? What is available at my destination? What comes in a light, small, unbreakable package? Do I have enough gifts for hosts and friends and others who favor me with kindnesses? What can be used for more than one purpose? In general, what is essential for my life in these special circumstances?

In *The Island of Dr. Death and Other Stories*, Gene Wolfe wrote about traveling: "Everyone takes what is necessary . . . it is what is taken that could be left behind that reveals the heart." I usually take more ballpoint pens than anyone could use and more chocolate than is good for me. What about you?

Travel forces me to prepare in other ways, too. Have my reservations been made in time? What deadlines will fall during my trip? Have lecture and workshop arrangements been properly delegated? Who will greet, transport, brief, feed, and house me? Who will help present constructive living by word and example to those who participate? If I should become ill or die, are my affairs in order? Who would carry on in my absence?

Travel requires that I look at my use of time in airports, in lines, in hotels, and elsewhere. Usually, I carry reading material, writing material, a laptop computer, blank postcards and water-colors, snacks, and a small tape recorder with tapes so that the hours won't be lost "in between" destinations. Watching, listening, and dozing require no special equipment. The true destination is always just here, now.

There is much to notice when traveling. Change of place heightens my sensitivity to scenery, customs, food, and expectations. Contrast helps me become aware of what I take for granted.

Robert Heinlein had a practical character in one of his fine novels remark that since his army days he never passed up the chance to sleep, eat, or urinate. There is much to be said for such advice. The luxury of travel steers us to the basics.

To be sure, we are all travelers all the time.

## No Solution to a Pseudo Problem

Neurosis is as natural as living. Because we live, we have desires and hopes. Because we have desires and hopes, we have fears of failing to achieve them in the future and memories of having failed to achieve them in the past.

How can we handle these anticipatory fears and discouraging memories? How can we cope with the reality that our desires and dreams always extend beyond our ability to attain them? One coping strategy is to try to pound down the desires to fit our capabilities, to try to achieve some merging of what we want with what we can have. That strategy appears attractive, but it is impossible to carry out successfully. It inevitably involves lying to ourselves about what we desire. Life *always* implies desires that exceed realistic limits.

Another coping strategy is to try to extend our capabilities to match our desires. Diligent study and hard work and striving for success may bring some rewards, but the desires keep growing apace, too. They always outstrip our efforts to attain complete satisfaction. So this coping strategy, too, is impossible to carry out successfully. Though there is nothing wrong with making efforts to grow, learn, advance, succeed, we'll never achieve all we desire.

Neurosis *is* being caught by this discrepancy between what is desired and what is possible. Neurosis involves a misdirection of attention toward this inherently insoluble problem of life. Neurosis is misdirected effort to resolve an unresolvable dilemma. No amount of effort works satisfactorily; no direct approach to the problem succeeds. The neurotic struggle produces frustration and a turning inward to the feelings that accompany the struggle. Perhaps at least the feelings of anxiety about future desires being unsatisfied and the self-doubts and self-recriminations over past failures can be eliminated somehow. But, no. There, too, we hit the dead end of impossibility.

Neither the basic problem of the discrepancy between desires and capabilities nor the subproblem of the unpleasant feelings accompanying recognition of this discrepancy can be solved. What is there to do?

The remarkable key that allows us to escape from this dark closet of frustration is to give up on trying to solve the dilemma altogether. In other words, we recognize the discrepancy between what we want and who we are (what we can achieve) and accept it. We recognize the feelings of anxiety and inadequacy that come with living and accept them. There is no need to fight, no need to wish life were otherwise than it is. We are just fine as we are.

Once (not really once, but over and over again) we recognize the naturalness of this reality of discrepancy, we can get on about directing our attention and efforts toward doing what is possible. We can begin to live constructively and realistically within the limits and potentials that life offers us. There has been no problem all along except for the one we created in our mind. There is only a naturally expansive set of desires, a naturally limited set of abilities to achieve them, and a pressure to achieve them all anyway.

To be alive is to need, to succeed and to fail, to be sometimes anxious and sometimes confident, sometimes regretful and sometimes satisfied. Life is just fine like that.

Wishing life were otherwise is to step back into the dark confines of the pseudo problem with no solution. Accepting life as it is allows freedom to work on *real* problems and to find *real* solutions.

DAVID K. REYNOLDS

## *Human Problems and Advice*

It is rather surprising to me that everyone isn't more neurotic. Traveling on the road of oversensitivity seems to be quite a natural journey.

### A LETTER

A few years ago I received a letter from a troubled young lady. She had been unfaithful to her husband after years of an uneven marriage. She wanted to unburden herself. She wanted advice about what to do next. Edited excerpts from my reply follow. Some details have been changed to protect the anonymity of the correspondent.

In the back of the book *Constructive Living* are some maxims. One of them is: "Give and give until you wave goodbye." I believe that it is important to give yourself to your husband (with the same spirit you give yourself to your daughter) all the while you are deciding whether to leave or not. If you don't give yourself away and you do break up, there will always be doubts about yourself and about the possibilities for the marriage that you never realized.

What you did, you did. That is reality. That reality cannot be changed. What you are doing now is under your control, within the frame of your own sense of moral responsibility. Trying to figure it all out isn't necessary or even possible. You were attracted to another man; you got involved with him; you felt bad about it afterward. Do you think that understanding yourself in great detail will make the attraction go away? I think it is unlikely.

You do have some clear purposes that are evidenced in what you do. You want to give the best to your daughter. Do what is best for her. You want to succeed in your profession. Do your work well. When in doubt, examine your purposes. *Your* purposes. And then do what fits with your purposes. You aren't responsible for fitting your purposes to what you think are society's purposes or your husband's purposes or God's purposes or my purposes. But you *must* act in scrupulous accord with your own purposes. When you drift from them, you will be dissatisfied. Then come back to them. Drift, come back—it is the same in meditating, in writing, in life.

Beware of generalizations and abstractions about yourself. You wrote, "I've become a very dishonest person, and have begun to doubt my motivations with men." Your letter glowed with your effort to be honest. You are not honest or dishonest; like all of us, you are sometimes this, sometimes that. And your motivations with men vary from man to man, from moment to moment. The point is to "do" this moment well, and this moment, and this moment. Then life seems to take care of itself.

I often remind myself that Morita never promised that his life-way would lead to success, but that we could learn to keep trying even as we fail.

A QUESTION

At a group meeting in Nagoya, Japan, a middle-aged man asked me what to do about his habit of watching staid documentary programs on educational television. He wanted to watch dramas and

DAVID K. REYNOLDS

comedies, too, but always ended up turning to the public educational channels.

I made a gesture of turning the channel selector on a television set and told him that was the solution to his problem. Everyone laughed. He understood.

People may desire an easier way. They may hope for some rational understanding that will make their problem readily disappear. They may seek a hint, a trick that will resolve their dilemma. But when there is no easy course, there is still a strategy that works. It is to change what we do—hurting or not, comfortable or not, anxious or not.

The fellow in Nagoya doesn't need to work on his compulsion to watch educational television programs. He doesn't need to examine the pressures his parents put on him during childhood to avoid "frivolous" pastimes. All he needs to do is switch channels to view a program he really wants to watch. There will be some initial discomfort, then his attention will be pulled into the drama on the screen and his problem will be gone for the moment. Should it reappear, he knows the solution for it. It takes just a turn of the wrist.

ANOTHER LETTER

A young lady in Japan wrote to me about her problems with her boyfriend of four years. He met with her only at his whim, taking a year off from the relationship at one time. Perhaps she wanted to know how to successfully bring him to a commitment of marriage, though she didn't write so directly.

If she succeeded in bringing him to the altar, I suspect she would be stuck with a disappointing married life. To lose him seems like throwing away four years of youth and waiting. But to win him may make the years ahead more difficult than they need to be.

Her letter reminded me of another young lady who waited eight years while her sweetheart worked in a remote part of the country. When he was finally transferred back to Tokyo, he broke up with her.

There may be hidden purposes for these women who wait and endure. They may be fearful of finding anyone else. They may be enraptured by family or social values of faithfulness, images of the "one and only" true love in life. Waiting or not is their choice. Whichever they choose, it is vitally important to know their purpose, accept their feelings, and do their choice well without complaint or dwelling on wishes that life were otherwise. And, of course, those who choose to wait can choose to stop waiting.

## HAVING YOUR CAKE AND EATING IT, TOO

I counseled a young lady who was upset and confused about her life. Her job would soon end, a divorce was in the offing, and she was having what she recognized as a silly affair with a self-destructive alcoholic who would move away in a couple of weeks. Furthermore, she had no immediate prospects for a new job, her rent on an expensive apartment would run out in a month, and she hadn't slept for two days.

As she told me her story, she was understandably tearful. She wondered what courses she might take or what meditative practice she might start to get her mind in shape to work on her problems. I told her she didn't need to wait to get her mind in shape. She could get going on some action that was necessary with her mind as it was.

I asked her to begin listing what needed doing—get some sleep, get information about job opportunities, check out less expensive housing, and so forth. She added to the list phone calls she needed to make, daily physical exercise, a talk with her current supervisor, and inquiries into storage for her property in another state.

I pointed out to her that as she wrote the list her tears were gone, her face was animated, bright. Each time she brought up her regrets about the dilemma in which she had placed herself, she became sad and tearful again. Each time she turned her attention

DAVID K. REYNOLDS

to the making a list of what she could do about her situation, her face turned back to businesslike determination. Even the listing itself seemed to have a beneficial, indirect influence on her feelings.

You can't control your feelings directly by your will, but you can act constructively in spite of them. And the wonderful fringe benefit of acting constructively is that feelings usually settle down as you accomplish your tasks. Anyway, while you wait for the misery to decline, why not get that room cleaned up?

### IT ISN'T BROKEN; DON'T TRY TO FIX IT

In one of my workshops a man was willing to accept that a certain degree of anxiety was all right, but he wanted some "cure" for the top 10 percent of his anxiety. A lady was willing to accept that her fear of flying was all right, but she wanted to pretend that she was floating in water rather than sitting on an airplane, in order to feel less fearful. Constructive living is about reality. Visualization and desensitization are useful crutches in the initial stages of getting done what needs doing in life, but acceptance of reality is the final goal.

The danger of mental crutches is that sometimes they work (temporarily, but with relief). Then we run the risk of becoming feeling-centered again. The payoff in life is greatest for the purpose-centered person. Visualization (imagining that you are where you aren't) may work now and then, but it's not a game you can win consistently. The game of pretending is aimed at fixing anxiety. But the anxiety doesn't need to be fixed. Constructive living is aimed at your getting done what reality brings you to do, anxious or not. *That's* a game you can win with great consistency.

## On Security

How insecure our lives are! We don't know if our products will continue to sell well. We have no assurance that our management decisions will turn out well. We cannot be certain that the person we love will continue to love us, or that our love for him or her will endure as it is now. We could get some dreadful terminal disease. An earthquake or accident or fire or lawsuit or tornado could wipe out our possessions and/or our lives.

Of course, we do what we can to protect ourselves and our loved ones and our possessions. But reality offers no guarantees.

The other day I caught my mind trying to avoid coming up with new ideas, new applications for constructive living. It was as though my mind believed that there was a limited number of ideas in some bag of creativity out there in the universe. It worried that if I drew too heavily on that supply of ideas, it would eventually be depleted. So, in order to protect my interests, my mind was making efforts to keep me from writing. It pointed me to the fifteen or so books of mine already in print. Could there possibly be anything more that I need to write?

But wisdom is limitless. Wisdom isn't mine. I am just a way some ideas get communicated to people. I borrow from this limitless bag of creativity that doesn't belong to me. I appreciate my mind's concern about the future, its attempts to ration my thinking

DAVID K. REYNOLDS

so that it will last longer. But the concern is misplaced. Just like our concerns about security.

Absolute security is impossible in this world. Businesses fail. Spouses die. We grow old, ill. We die. Our treasures and economies are undependable. Quarrels and wars and economic depressions and natural disasters of all kinds loom ready to pounce on our peace of mind.

Security can only exist now. The future offers no real promises. To do very well, with full attention, what lies before me now is my only chance for guaranteed success. It isn't that my efforts now will result in success tomorrow. My diligent efforts now *are* success.

So I keep on writing, never knowing when my connection with that fund of ideas will shrivel up like some newborn's umbilical cord. Writing now, only now.

# The Truth of the Matter

For a while we believed that truth was relative—that anything somebody believed was true for him or her and, so, equal in truth value for everyone.

That's wrong.

On pragmatic grounds, that attitude allows a child with curable pneumonia to be treated by a witch doctor or not at all, depending on the religious beliefs of the child's parents. The child who could have been saved by antibiotics may die.

But in another sense, no matter what my friend Carlos Castaneda writes, no matter what theoretical physicists write about space within and between atoms, every time I thump my hand against this desk, my hand hits solid reality. It hurts.

I'm not interested in debating philosophically about what is "really real." Morita wrote that "reality is truth." (Jijitsu yuishin.) Did you hang up your clothes or not? Did you get up promptly or not? Did you take the vacation or not? That's the simpleminded reality I want to talk about. All the talk about motivation and addictive personality and mental readiness and decision making and positive thinking are ephemeral wisps compared to the truth of reality. The truth is right before your eyes. The game playing goes on in your mind. No matter how skillfully you present your case, reality shows the truth. Pay attention to it.

A young lady who sat in one of my New York workshops showed a remarkable pattern of behavior. She would raise a question, then, when I answered it, she would say, "In other words, you . . ." and then she would complete her sentence with something far from what I had said. I would try to correct her only to hear her say, "In other words, you . . ." and again she would grossly misinterpret my words. Finally, I got tired of her game and called it off. I don't know what her purpose was in mishearing. Others in the auditorium seemed to be understanding, at least on the surface. I don't often use difficult words when I speak or write. Perhaps the lady wished to hear something she could dismiss so that she could avoid wrestling with her current view of the world.

But whatever her purpose, she wasn't attending to reality. She wasn't listening. Others were, and they told her so. Reality was teaching her something, but she may not have been learning.

These days many people think that they can afford to spend a great deal of time escaping from reality. Some might even read this book as they would read a novel, to entertain themselves and get their minds off the reality that confronts them. That approach would be a pity. They might say, Ah, yes, how interesting a point of view! Then they could turn to the next film or television program or novel or lecture and escape into that. How sad for them!

This constructive living can help you take more interest in your real life! Your everyday life holds much more that's worth your attention than you may have thought. Reality is inherently fascinating. But you may need to unclutter your mind, to discard some useless mental baggage in order to notice reality. Proper simplification will free up your attention to see that reality is truth, indeed!

Words, words. We try to use them to give a taste, a glimpse, a direction. Something is there. The danger is that hearing, you think that you know what that something is. You don't understand just by hearing or reading. Only by effortful doing and by the resultant experiencing can you understand at last. And the understanding will come in little oozes and squirts, not often in floods.

## Co-writing the Scripts of Our Lives

We don't write the scripts of our lives alone. For all our diligent scripting, reality comes along and throws our plots out the window. Life never quite works out the way we had planned.

Nevertheless, when reality asks us a question, we can write our response to that question. We get to write our part, but only as it fits within the whole play, reality's play. We are central characters only to ourselves and to those close to us.

I used to think of the garden as a personal challenge—the weeds versus me. Now the weeding is just something else needing to be done—by somebody, sometimes me. Reality keeps teaching that I am not on center stage. It keeps moving *me* out of its march.

Not long ago I watched a drunken Japanese laborer, *tabi* boots and *hachimaki* tied around his head, struggling to climb up the slippery side of a children's slide in a playground in Ueno Park. When he reached the top of the slide, he stood swaying for a moment, then he tried to slide down while standing upright. Part of the way down, he fell to a sitting position. He ended lying on his back on the ground. He leaped to his feet and began energetically climbing the slippery slide again. Whatever his goals and means, his persistence deserves applause, I thought.

**DAVID K. REYNOLDS**

A rape victim came for training in constructive living. She was trying to hang all her past on one hanger, her rape experience. It can't be done. There are lots of hangers in the closets of our pasts· our first romance, our first lie, our first act of cowardice, our first act of unselfish giving, menses and wet dreams and so on and on. No single event or experience determines who we are.

Walking in a forest in upstate New York, I noticed that some tall evergreen trees had leaves only near their crowns. The branches below were black and bare for twenty or thirty feet right to the ground. Perhaps insects or disease or lack of sunlight caused the blighted condition of the trees' past. Those trees were green and living in the now, though, despite their tragic past. Such a life is possible for sexually abused children, too.

Every once in a while reality writes a *deai* into our life scripts. Perhaps the best translation of the Japanese word *deai* would be "encounter." But the word in Japanese carries implications of an important encounter that involves a turning point in life. There must be some situation that spontaneously puts one in touch with some circumstance—most often, some person—who will have a strong influence in the writing of one's life script.

However, the circumstance of encounter is not sufficient for a *deai* to occur. There must be personal preparation and a readiness to recognize the opportunity in order for a *deai* to take place. We miss some potential *deai* in our lives because we aren't ready for them. When the well-known Moritist Takehisa Kora was a young man, it was said of him that his head was in the clouds so much he should become an astronomer. Fortunately, in spite of his daydreaming ways, he was sufficiently prepared to recognize his *deai* with Morita.

One of the ways we can defend ourselves from disastrous detours written into the scripts of our lives is to create a multitude of tasks, hopes, interests, backups, and facets of character so that if one area of life fails, other areas remain. Risking all our satisfaction and self-esteem on one narrow field of living invites trouble. Responding to what reality brings us, we still have some control over the variety of scenes, scenery, and staging in which we play out our lives  One of my students came up with the word *selfation*. It means "we save ourselves through our own efforts." That's true, but only half the truth. The other truth is that reality keeps saving us, too, through the concrete efforts of others in our lives. People teach and feed and clothe and shelter us. They provide attention and love and information and examples and gas for the car. Not only people but nonpeople things save us. Oxygen, water, electricity, the sun, plants, and so on are written into our life scripts by reality.

They (and we) are all part of the grand play.

DAVID K. REYNOLDS

# The Dignity of Reality

I suppose starry skies are majestic and newborn babies are miracles to just about everybody. How about fingernails and crabgrass and ice on the windshield and plastic ware? Are they worthy of wonder? Ask a child.

It seems that I'm about to pass a kidney stone. Reality brings discomfort . . . and doctors and nurses and X rays and fluids and a body that carries out its usual functions while dealing with this added factor. Every once in a while, the awesome nature of it all hits me. Reality goes on about its business, presenting now this and now that. Impressive.

In my youth I had difficulties understanding the dignity of humankind. Certainly, some of the people I saw on the streets weren't dignified. And the horrors some humans inflicted on other humans seem to make the race as a whole unworthy of any blanket dignity.

I had equal trouble distinguishing between self-respect and conceit. On the one hand I was told I must have pride in myself. On the other hand I was taught that the meek shall inherit the earth. Stand tall but be humble.

There is a path out of that maze of paradox. We humans take our dignity from reality. We are part of that awesome reality, and we alone have flashes of recognition of reality's wonder. It is not me (as an individual or as a representative of humanity) who is particularly valuable, but me-as-part-of-this-momentary-reality that is special. So are you.

As I wrote in *Even in Summer the Ice Doesn't Melt,* I am sometimes this, sometimes that. We are all sometimes generous sometimes miserly, sometimes giving sometimes taking, sometimes kind sometimes cruel. It is our status as reality's representatives that makes us humans of extraordinary worth. We take on our dignity as a gift borrowed from reality, never separable from this-reality-now.

As usual, those readers with traditional religious backgrounds should have little trouble substituting other words for *reality* in the paragraphs above—God, for example.

I have been asked if constructive living is a Buddhist lifeway. I think that it is no more Buddhist than Judeo-Christian, and that it is neither. It is based on something more fundamental than religious Buddhism or religious Christianity. It is based on a fundamental understanding of the human mind's operating system. Western psychology has taught us little about the operation of the human mind. The attempts to make psychology, sociology, and anthropology "scientific" have doomed academics to a sort of "human science" parody. As they imitate the formal methods of the physical sciences, these social scientists teach us little more than their virtuosity at experimental design. Akegarasu wrote: "Don't ask me why: I don't know why. But everything I see is living and dancing. I deeply pity those smart people who use their own paltry understanding of nature to kill nature and then bury themselves in its cold dead body."* There is wisdom in his words.

Introspection, insight, a phenomenological perspective are essential to any true understanding of that flow of awareness that constitutes our existence. There is a tradition of Buddhism, Sufism, Taoism, mystical Judaism, and mystical Christianity (to name a few) with recorded introspective experimentation. There have been people who invested years of their lives watching their minds function. Their wisdom should not be ignored.

*Akegarasu, 1977, p. 98

DAVID K. REYNOLDS

Constructive living strips away some of the cultural/religious trappings from these fundamental insights into the mind. Constructive living reinterprets these insights in terms more palatable to the modern rational intellect without rendering them impotent. The intellectual aspect is balanced by the experiential aspect. Teaching is balanced by exercises. Theory is balanced by tales and personal experiment. Always, always comes the advice: Check out what constructive living suggests against your own experience. Don't compare it with what you have been taught in formal education classes or what some historical figure has theorized. Compare this understanding with your life experience, and accept only the part that makes sense to you here, now. Then keep on tacking down what you believe to what you experience. Eventually, you will discard a great deal of memorized debris and get down to insights worth building your life upon in this moment and the next.

# The First Mistake of My Life

I misused a word in Japanese and, when corrected, I told my friend that it was the first mistake I ever made. A bit later I misjudged the size of a package and couldn't fit it into the bag I had selected. Again, my friend heard that it was the first mistake of my life. My friend laughed. How could they both be the first mistake I ever made? Had I forgotten the blunder in Japanese just a few minutes before?

When we begin to see every moment as a fresh one, when we see ourselves changing moment by moment, making a mistake becomes less worrisome. It was an old me that slipped up in Japanese. And already it is a previous me that misjudged the size of the package. Reality keeps giving me fresh starts, fresh chances to make the first success or the first failure of this new life moment.

Mistakes can sometimes be avoided. There's a Japanese saying: "Wait three days, then quarrel." It is good advice. After three days, what seemed to be such a giant issue is likely to be seen in new perspective. We Westerners are too eager to put our feelings into immediate action. With the passage of time, we usually wonder at the foolishness of our earlier flare-ups. To be sure, there are times for immediate action, too. But most of my students need more work on waiting than on immediate responses. So do I.

Some mistakes are reflections of lack of gratitude. Unfolded pajamas reflect lack of proper respect for the services pajamas perform. Unshined shoes, an unmade bed, unwashed dishes or clothes are examples of ingratitude. They are mistakes, more important mistakes than may appear on the surface.

There is a kind of mistake that comes from doing well when there is something even better. On an episode of the television series *St. Elsewhere* (February 18, 1987), a young doctor confronted the prison inmate who raped him and said, "I'm not afraid of you anymore." That is fine if true. Better still would be to say, "I'm afraid of you, but that doesn't stop me from testifying against you." Can you see the difference? The fear may come and go. But the firm commitment to the right action takes precedence over the fear. Whatever happens with the fear, he can do what needs to be done.

Now, the truly oversensitive person, on reading this discussion about mistakes, will begin to ruminate about mistakes. His or her thinking may go something like this: I make too many mistakes. There must be some way to cut down on them. Even the things that seem to be going well are probably mistakes on some higher level. And I rush into things, making even more mistakes. What can I do?

The constructive-living solution to such rumination is to allow the obsession to continue as long as it does. Meanwhile, get up and do dishes, bake, wash your car, whatever. Notice how the overconcern with mistakes drifts away as you get involved in some constructive activity. We all lean a little forward as we walk.

# Morality

Both the Morita therapy and Naikan elements of constructive living require us to view every act as having moral implications. The way we wash our face, the way we take off our socks, the way we use dishwashing liquid—all are moral acts that can be sinful or righteous. Again, there is no behavior free from moral valuation. The smallest act carries implications about the development of our character for good or for evil, for constructive or destructive purposes. Feelings, you recall, aren't controllable directly by the will, so they don't carry the same moral implications as behavior.

Let's consider folding socks. Emi Ogawa, the wife of Dr. Brian Ogawa (a Morita therapist in Hawaii) has solved the sock koan. Emi Ogawa has demonstrated the best way to fold socks that I have ever seen. The socks are folded together and turned partway inside out without stretching. Then when it is time to wear them, one simply inserts the foot into the front of the sock and pulls the rest over the heel and up the ankle. Emi Ogawa's careful consideration of an ordinary life situation has turned sock folding into an art, a moral act in the sense used above. From this description, can you duplicate Emi Ogawa's solution to the sock koan?

One of my favorite periodicals is the *Foghorn*. Few would view any obvious moral implications of the publication. The Fog organization provides a wealth of elegant solutions to practical CPM

DAVID K. REYNOLDS

and DOS operating systems computer problems. Enthusiasts have invested time and effort in solving computer difficulties, then they freely share those solutions with others. They exhibit some of the finest human qualities—persistence, carefulness, intelligence, and generosity. Morality is not limited to Sunday mornings and church services. It is interwoven throughout the way we live.

Talking about constructive living is rather like hearing sports figures interviewed. Their talk is nothing compared to their performance.

# The Truth About Psychotherapy

Aren't you *tired* of it? All the feeling, feeling, feeling stuff? Don't you long to go beyond it? To get beyond the self-centered, self-seeking, self-building, self-displaying selfishness? Don't you yearn to get beyond the profit-loss mentality and the shallow nostalgia and the paper-thin patriotism of us against them?

At last, people seem to be seeking realism, but realism of a special sort—ground-down, rounded realism, the kind that comes from enduring while keeping the eyes open, not running away when life becomes a bit uncomfortable. Some of us are tired of airy idealism and mystic wordmaking. Our preferences are being recognized in the psychotherapies that have emerged in recent years. Psychotherapy is, after all, distilled knowledge about how to live.

Psychotherapy is an art. Like any art, it has its fashions and movements. Ten years ago, the concepts of constructive living seemed quite radical in light of the emphasis on focusing on feelings, analyzing them, and expressing them. Nowadays the emphasis on accepting feelings while maintaining behavioral responsibility seems much less radical. Western psychotherapy has incorporated some constructive-living ideas as though they were

DAVID K. REYNOLDS

always there in full-blown form. Recently, I read a book, *Feel the Fear and Do It Anyway!*, by Susan Jeffers. The title could have come from Japan's turn-of-the-century Morita therapy, a major component of constructive living. There are important differences between Jeffers's approach and constructive living (she emphasizes the diminishing fears that follow action, for example), but the notion that feelings need not push around our behavior is similar.

Lakin Phillips's excellent book, *A Guide for Therapists and Patients to Short-Term Psychotherapy*, was reviewed by Richard K. McGee in *Contemporary Psychology* in equally perceptive fashion.

I quote here from McGee's review:

> Few intellectually honest practitioners have ever touted psychotherapy as a scientific endeavor; most have believed the practice of therapy is an art. . . . Psychotherapy is a business, operating in a competitive market, with enlightened consumers who expect to receive value and quality for their health dollars. . . .
> The reader who might be contemplating therapy will learn several important facts about the industry in which he or she may be about to invest time and money. First, the history of psychotherapy began with a form of treatment in which hundreds of hours were spent in the process. Second, there is no solid evidence that psychoanalysis (or the many modifications of it that have evolved over the years) accomplishes anything significant in the real-life behavior of the client. Third, most of the really important benefits of therapy occur early in the process and continue even if the client discontinues regular visits to the therapist. Fourth, therapists may have their own personal and professional motives for prolonging the therapeutic enterprise, not the least of which are financial. Fifth, the real reason for entering into therapy, and the bottom-line criterion of its success, is to effect some change in the client's behavior as he or she interacts with life. Sixth, financial assistance is available for psychotherapy if one is willing to endure a formal diag-

nosis, which has little functional value beyond helping the patient to collect insurance benefits. Finally, patients may avoid the primarily commercial therapy ventures by maintaining an active, evaluative attitude before starting and while participating in the therapeutic process.

The reader would do well to consider McGee's words carefully. There is nothing magical about this joint endeavor called psychotherapy. It is built upon purposes, just as all human endeavors are. We must be clear about our purposes, whether we are therapists or clients, teachers or students.

Psychoanalytic therapy helps patients explore their purposes and offers the possibility of discovering alternate purposes and alternate ways of achieving their purposes. But that exploration alone is like sending a pitcher home after he has been warming up for the game in the bullpen. The work is yet to come.

In psychotherapeutic arts, almost any theory has some usefulness if both therapist and client believe in it. Theories offer some sense of organization and control over reality, whether the control actually exists or not. I am not particularly concerned with minor variations in constructive-living theory. I am concerned that my students act realistically and constructively. Lifeways may hold out grand goals of enlightenment and growth, but they must return the student's attention to reality if they are to give greatest benefit.

When the therapy fosters dependence on the therapist, it is self-limiting. One of my students got permission from his psychotherapist to try another form of therapy—that is, to come to see me. Permission, mind you.

Entrenched psychiatry departments stick to psychoanalysis and behavior therapy like they stick to IBM computers. They may not be the best and they may not be the most cost effective, but they are a safe managerial choice.

The orientation sheet for a new student at the ToDo Institute clearly states that constructive living is not psychotherapy. It is a form of reeducation, a lifeway. But McGee's caution and advice apply all the same. The measure of constructive living's success is the positive change effected in our behavior as we "interact with life," as we participate in the ever-changing dance of reality.

It is time that psychotherapists stop pretending they know what they don't really know. The mind remains mysterious. Let us acknowledge its mystery and get on with constructive lives. It isn't necessary (or possible) to exhaustively probe the depths of the mind in order to proceed with a good life.

Please remember that I don't write so that you will say, "How interesting!" but so that you will change what you do.

# Levels of One Dimension
## of Human Development

Cleaning occurs, gratitude occurs

I clean in order to clean, pride occurs

I clean my messy room to distract myself from feelings

I escape from my distress by reading a novel

I don't clean my messy room and am distressed by it

I don't clean my messy room and don't notice it

We don't stay on any stage permanently. Rather, we move up and down as our life practice develops and slows.

The first four steps are feeling-centered, the next is purpose-centered, the top step is reality-centered.

## Constructive Living and an Eating Disorder

My student was an attractive twenty-three year-old Japanese female, NT, who worked in a large company analyzing documents. She lived with her father, mother, and younger brother in a city not far from Tokyo. She weighed 39.5 kg and was 155 cm tall. She remembered herself as being somewhat overweight in high school. She smoked about ten cigarettes per day. Her presenting problem began when she was about twenty-two years old.

At that time she wanted to become slim so she ate little and lost quite a bit of weight. She began to have periods of binge eating that lasted two or three days each. Her most recent binge lasted three days and included chocolate bars after breakfast, no eating during the morning hours at work, lunch, no eating during the afternoon at work, more chocolate, dinner, and late eating of uncooked refrigerated foods before bed. She feared to begin eating at all because the taste of spicy, oily, or sweet foods seemed to stimulate binges. She had no history of vomiting; she suffered from mild constipation. Her family knew of her problem, but her workmates didn't. She felt anxiety when offered food during breaks at work and when invited to join others for meals.

NT had lived three years in the United States, attending high school there. She returned to Japan for college, graduating with a major in physical science. Having lived in the United States, NT was dissatisfied with some aspects of Japan, but she felt at home in neither place. She was bright and sensitive in character. When she came for constructive-living training, she was taking tranquilizing medication prescribed by the referring Japanese psychiatrist.

I believe that all behavior is purposeful. One of the primary goals of therapy is to discover the latent purposes of neurotic habits in order to find alternate ways of achieving those purposes and to set new goals in place of existing purposes. One of the purposes of NT's eating disorder seemed to be to prevent her from having to become an adult.

To NT, adulthood meant being perfect (like her father), without fault or weakness, it meant separation from her parents, working at an uninteresting job until marriage, finding and attracting an eligible male, then living an uninteresting married life. It is no wonder that with this view of adulthood NT was taking pains to avoid it.

Several homework assignments were made during the first session. NT was to keep a journal for several days, providing an objective account of what she had eaten and in what quantities. She was to accompany her father to his regular tennis-club outing and offer encouragement and nurturance to him. In other words, she was to observe while her father made the usual mistakes of an amateur tennis player, and to practice supporting him in a sort of role reversal. Finally, she was to eat the foods she wished and to advise her mother that her therapist recommended against trying to force foods on NT. This assignment took off some of the pressure from her mother and put responsibility for eating back in NT's hands.

NT failed to appear for our second session, having misremembered the date. At the third session, NT weighed 38.5 kg. She had had one evening of binge eating during the intervening sixteen days. On that day she ate an ordinary breakfast and lunch, then, between 2 and 5 P.M. she ate four small chocolate snacks, one box of cookies, four small Japanese sandwiches, french fried potatoes, potato chips, a piece of apple pie, and four pieces of

DAVID K. REYNOLDS

candy. After a light dinner she ate four small pastries, a container of yogurt, and a piece of soft candy. The next day she ate lightly. She had maintained a careful record of all her food intake each day since our first session, as assigned.

At this session, NT remarked that her father watched food programs on television, enjoyed eating, and suggested menus to her mother. When NT tried to talk with her father about his facade of perfection, he told her that men don't expose their weaknesses and failures to women. It seemed clear to both of us that her eating disorder was related to her relationship with her father. She was troubled in the very area of life that brought him great pleasure. She resisted my suggestion that she was already an adult, responsible for what she ate. One of her goals continued to be to remain a child so that she need not be an adult like her father.

She saw some progress in these two sessions. Her assignments included polishing her father's shoes, getting him a lap blanket when it is cold, and creating a design for the family's New Year cards (leaving the selection and decision about the design to her father). It may seem strange to the Western reader to assign such services in this case. However, in serving her father, she develops her own strength and self-image as one who gives. In bringing him a blanket, she acknowledges his need for warmth. In shining his dirty shoes, she must again notice his imperfection. In this case I had no permission or time to work with the family, so I could not assign complementary tasks to her father.

At this time we terminated our sessions, because I was to return to the United States later that week. NT had my telephone number and address in Los Angeles. She promised to stay in touch through the winter until my trip to Japan the following spring.

A Christmas card informed me, "I am very grateful for what you taught me, and I'm giving my best effort to be who I'd like to be. I'm doing quite well these days!"

Follow-up six months later showed stable weight and no binges, though NT continued her oversensitivity to food-related behavior. She was active in skiing and yachting. NT had discovered an attractive male. However, she had begun quarreling with her mother over the inconvenience her food preferences caused. Mother and daughter were seen separately for one session each. The emphasis of our discussions was on practical behaviors that would resolve immediate difficulties (such as having NT assist with buying groceries and food preparation) and on the impossibility of achieving perfectionistic ideals. Again, my return to the U.S. brought an end to our sessions.

Follow-up one year later showed no binge eating during the previous year.

# Hard and Soft Morita
## Guidance

### INTRODUCTION

Constructive living is an original composition based largely on elements from two Japanese lifeways, Morita therapy and Naikan. In this short essay, we shall think about polar extremes in the teaching styles of constructive living. I consider them to be reflections of the hard-line and the soft-line interpretations of Moritist thought and practice. Constructive-living guides develop their own styles of teaching this lifeway to their students. Moreover, they may vary their styles to meet the changing needs of particular students over a course of guidance or to reflect the development of their own constructive life at any point in time. As we shall see, my own preference is toward the hard line; but that is not to say I consider that end of the continuum correct or advanced in some respect. It is nothing more than a matter of personal style. In this essay, I have drawn the extremes more clearly than they exist in reality, perhaps. In actual practice, there is blurring and mixing of tactics as seems necessary.

Put briefly, the soft approach emphasizes understanding, expression, explanation, and a personal relationship with the teacher. The hard approach emphasizes acceptance, endurance, advice, exercises, and a personal relationship with reality. Those who practice the soft approach don't ignore the elements of acceptance, endurance, advice, exercises, and the teachings of reality. However, they use understanding, expression, explanation, and their human relationship as intermediate, expedient means for teaching the hard-line truths.

Soft-line teachers see hard-liners as requiring unnecessarily ascetic discipline from their students. Why require a steep course when there is an easier course available? Why not utilize culturally acceptable methods and expectations to facilitate the teaching?

Hard-line teachers see soft-liners as treading potentially dangerous trails. The course may be easy, but the soft-liners run the risk of taking their students in undesirable directions. Let us look at some of the similarities and differences between the extreme styles and the thinking that underlies them.

## THE SOFT LINE

The soft line fits the expectations of Western students. It approximates a counseling form of psychotherapy. Sessions begin with a sympathetic and empathetic therapist listening to the symptom complaints of the client. The constructive-living guide has in mind goals of motivating the student to learn and carry out constructive-living assignments. The guide also models acceptance of the clients with the goal of helping the clients accept and validate themselves. Clearly, clients come wanting to be understood and accepted, wanting to find some comforting technique that will help them understand and deal with their symptoms. The soft-line guide accommodates the clients' desires at this early stage of counseling.

This style of teaching utilizes explanation as an important aid in engendering the students' cooperation. Students want to know why they are suffering. They want to know why a particular assignment has been given. They believe that intellectual under-

**DAVID K. REYNOLDS**

standing will be of benefit in their practice of constructive-living principles. Western students may resist exercises that don't make sense to them. Just as Western patients want to know what medicines their physicians have prescribed and why, so our students want to know what is going on in the course of their education in constructive living.

The soft-line guide considers some expression of feelings as a cathartic release and a help in assisting students to recognize and accept their feelings. Students should be permitted the opportunity to vent their feelings provided they don't complain excessively. Once the students have exhausted their own expressive repertoires, they are ready to hear what the guide has to teach. Trying to teach while the student is filled with rage or frustration or sorrow or whatever is a difficult and unrewarding task.

In sum, the soft-line guide sees intellectual understanding, expression of feelings, and explanation of constructive-living principles to be useful aids in teaching the basics of this lifeway. After all, why put off students with a hard-line approach when these tactics can make the teaching more palatable and more effective? Such is the pragmatic view of the soft-liner.

## THE HARD LINE

The hard-line guide may be seen as an idealist by some, but the approach is fundamentally pragmatic. From the hard-line perspective, intellectual understanding of neurotic lifeways through rational explanation is simply impossible—at best a sort of mind game that pacifies the intellect. No one understands why we do what we do. No one understands why feelings emerge at particular times with particular intensities. Beyond some superficial, common sense-level recognition of our thoughts, feelings, and behaviors and their probable causes there is no understanding possible or necessary. The hard-liner doubts that anyone knows what motivation is at all. The reality is that a student does assignments or doesn't do them, appears for a session or doesn't appear. Some students who appear highly motivated don't follow through. Others who appear unmotivated actually carry out assignments and exercises. To offer, after the fact, in-depth psychology explanations of "symptoms" or "motivation" is not only to provoke misunderstanding, but results in more focus on the "symptoms" and other presumed mental processes themselves. The hard-liners cannot offer explanations of what they themselves don't pretend to understand in themselves or in their students. Rather than explanations, they offer advice and assignments based on their experience.

There is no way to teach self-understanding or self-validation or self-acceptance verbally. It exists or it doesn't. There is no way that a guide can model pure acceptance of the student, because the guide's acceptance of the student (or even of the guide himself or herself) varies from moment to moment. Acceptance, the *arugamama* ("as it is") acceptance of constructive living, must be attained through the students' effortful action on reality.

Similarly, expression of feelings may provide some temporary relief from the pressure, or it may provoke more feelings and destructive circumstances that stimulate more feelings. For example, throwing a dish at a spouse may express feelings at the cost of the spouse's retaliation, trips to an emergency clinic, guilt, and so forth. Expression of feelings within the teaching setting validates the importance of feelings in the eyes of guide and student. It isn't that feelings are unimportant within the constructive lifeway, but they are clearly subordinate to proper attentive action—subordinate because actions are directly controllable, while feelings are not. Overemphasis on feelings distorts our perception of the whole reality that presents itself to us. More than expression, endurance is likely to bring about the benefits the students desire. Enduring feelings while continuing with constructive action teaches lessons about feelings' fading over time and the possibility of building life on controllable behavior. Acceptance and endurance put feelings in their proper perspective. Expression, even verbal expression, of feelings is likely to magnify their importance.

The hard-liner holds that talk is unlikely to provide much help to the student. Progress will come through the student's diligent practice of assignments and exercises. That behavior will result in experiential understanding and life change. Assignments and exercises provide the situational soil for the natural healthy growth of a constructive life. In this sense, the important factor promoting growth is nature or reality. The role of the guide is minimized. The student's actions on reality provide the teaching. Reality is the true guide. The hard-liners see themselves as merely "fingers pointing at the moon." The finger is not the moon.

## SUMMARY

In the following chart are outlined the major similarities and differences between the hard line and the soft line of constructive living with regard to a characteristic issue, feelings. Of course, both styles recognize the value of recognition and acceptance of feelings. Both styles use assignments to teach experientially validated truths. Both styles aim to offer the students a new perspective on life. Hard-liners aren't hard-hearted, and soft-liners aren't soft-headed. They use whatever seems needed in order to accomplish their purposes.

### Feelings

| Soft Line | Hard Line |
| --- | --- |
| Recognize | Recognize |
| Understand | Accept |
| Accept | |
| | |
| Express | Endure |
| Accept | Accept |
| | |
| Explain | Advise |
| Assign exercises | Assign exercises |

# Compulsions

Compulsions are one kind of *toraware*, that narrowed, fixed, frozen, obsessed state of mind that contrasts with natural flowing reality-focused awareness.

## HANDWASHING

One of my students washes her hands again and again at home. She has no trouble with compulsive handwashing outside the home. I advised her to select each morning the number of times she will wash her hands that day. She might start with twenty or so and cut back until she is within a normal range.

I asked her to thank the water each time she uses it (feeling grateful to the water or not) and to keep a careful written record of each handwashing event. Her attention to water's contribution to her life may help her use it more carefully, to use it as a measured, treasured resource. The written record provides an objective account of her behavior.

This lady also worries that her hair has traces of shampoo in it, so she rinses it again and again. I doubted aloud that anyone ever died of shampoo in the hair. She laughed. I suggested that she set a fixed time for her bath and leave the bathing room at that time, whatever she feels about the unfinished business.

DAVID K. REYNOLDS

These artificial, self-imposed restrictions are first steps only. Just like the tactic of turning immediately to some other task in order to distract her from symptoms/bad habits, these tactics are helpful stepping-stones toward the constructive-living goal. But our final destination is not to wash hands a fixed number of times each day or to stay in the bath for a predetermined period of time. The ultimate goal is to wash hands only when they need to be washed and to bathe only as long as necessary. The goal is to be living naturally according to the situation and not according to some inflexible, obsessive whim.

## SELF-GROWTH

Some people feel a similar compulsion to attend self-growth lectures and workshops and seminars and, generally, to "work on themselves." I wrote about them in *Water Bears No Scars,* calling them wing junkies, who seek to fly the skies on the winged steed Satori. Of course, they can never mount the enlightenment stallion, because their focus is scattered and they wouldn't know a saddle if they saw one. Nevertheless, they feel driven to seek someone or something that will provide instant release, perfect peace, endless joy, and the like.

P was worried, at first, that she might be a self-growth junkie. But she persevered in her study of constructive living long enough to learn that this lifeway will inform everything she does from now on. So if she were to attend a conference on est or some other New Age teaching, she would participate in constructive-living fashion, with attention to details of reality, focus on purpose, acceptance of her feelings, straightforward action, and so forth. She can no longer completely abandon what she has learned about living from Morita and Yoshimoto. It is rather like having learned a language. She may forget some of the vocabulary and grammar, but there will remain some familiarity even should she put it aside for years. And P won't do that. She recognizes already the value of living constructively in this manner. In fact, she has begun teaching others about the constructive life-style.

# Naikan in Constructive Living

A hundred times a day I remind myself that my inner and out life depends on the labors of other men, living and dead, and that I must exert myself in order to give in the measure as I have received and am still receiving.

—Albert Einstein

Once upon a misguided time, there was a hungry child. Along came an adult carrying bread. The adult said to the child, "When you are hungry I suffer, too. Please, take this bread and eat it. I love you." The child took the bread and ate it gladly, and for a while the child wasn't hungry.

Time passed and the child became hungry again. An adult came along carrying bread. The adult said, "You never do what I tell you to do. I'm going to give you this bread. The next time I tell you to do something, remember who gave you this bread. You'll obey if you ever want bread again from me." The child ate the bread thoughtfully.

In time the child became hungry again. An adult passed by and left bread within reach of the child. The adult said nothing, seemed to take no notice of the child or the child's hunger. But the ignored child ate the bread and the hunger remained at bay for a period of time.

There are two truths to this story. Most of my suffering students see only the truth of the varied attitudes of the adults (parents, if you will). The first adult was loving, the second was controlling, and the third was indifferent. The other truth to the story is that all three adults brought bread for the child to eat, and the child ate.

For all the imperfections of those who reared us, there were people in our lives who fed us and changed our diapers and clothed us whether they were in the mood or not, whether we were grateful or not, whether it was convenient for them or not. We survived because of their efforts. We screamed when our needs weren't met at the level of our expectations, and we rarely considered thanking or serving them. Humans are the most helpless and self-centered of creatures when young. We require great attention and care as infants or we die. Such is reality.

We have been taught to focus on the faults and limitations of our parents and other significant others in our lives. We have been taught to see their misbehavior as the cause of our own. We can blame them for our hang-ups and deficiencies. How convenient for us. The other truth is forgotten.

Naikan is about recognizing how we "are lived," as the Japanese put it. The countless efforts of others supported us in the past and continue to support us in this very moment. Such recognition is not vague and abstract and philosophical. Naikan invites us to consider specific people who acted in particular ways within concrete situations to provide us with explicit services and objects.

Naturally, Naikan produces gratitude. But the gratitude is not some generalized thankfulness to the universe. Rather, it is focused gratitude, gratitude that spurs us to repay our debts to people and objects, and even to the electricity and gas and water in our homes. You can tell something about people's level of Naikan by observing how many paper towels they use in a public restroom or whether they leave the water running as they brush their teeth or how often they say or write thank you to their mother and father or what they do first when they come home from work. Naikan is not just about good feelings; it is about what we do.

Naikan permeates constructive living. The attitude of the guide is suffused with Naikan gratitude. If there were an absence of grateful acceptance while the guide listens, there would be grave danger of constructive living's becoming a moralistic, judgmental imparting of the guide's values on the student. It would no longer be constructive-living guidance.

As you read in an earlier chapter, Naikan is a systematic method for recalling the past. Beginning with memories of the mother (or mother surrogate), Naikan students reflect on 1) what was received; 2) what was returned; and 3) troubles the student caused that person. Periodically, the student communicates with the Naikan guide about the recollections. The guide listens gratefully, without judgment or interpretation. After Naikan on the mother is completed, the student begins again with the father and other important people in the student's life. In the United States, we move then from reflections on people we know to reflections on people whose names we don't know. The driver who stopped for us at a crosswalk, the waitress who mopped up our spilled water, and the service-station attendant who washed our windshield are examples of such people. Then we move on to the specific contributions of other living creatures, objects, and energy in our lives. We move in this sequence from the familiar to the wider rings of support that surround us. But on all levels we look for the concrete and specific services and gifts and troubles.

One of the results of Naikan is a shift in perspective from emphasis on making sure our own needs are met to doing what we can to meet the needs of others. When we permit our mothers to control us, for example, the bitter struggle over who is in the driver's seat disappears. For her sake, in repayment for the years of service (bread) she gave us, there is submission. And then, for her sake, it is possible to resist and develop our independence, too. If our struggle for independence is suffused with selfish purpose, the results will be disappointing. The balance comes not when our

DAVID K. REYNOLDS

needs are satisfactorily met but when we are intent on seeing that our mothers' genuine needs are met. While submitting, we can teach the act of loving self-sacrifice to the very people who in all likelihood modeled such loving self-sacrifice to us in the first place. In the resistance we can teach the lesson of acting to meet the genuine needs of another in spite of the discomfort it may cause us and her temporarily. It's all in the purpose, the intent.

Of course, Naikan applies not only to our mothers. Unfolded pajamas means lack of proper gratitude toward the pajamas. Un-shined shoes, an unmade bed, unwashed dishes are examples of the same principle. With Naikan, we properly care for those objects that serve us just as we properly care for the people in our lives. The pull for such action is spontaneous appreciation and gratitude; the push for such action is spontaneous guilt when we fail to repay as we should. Both guilt and gratitude are wonderful, positive forces that merit appreciation as well.

# Relationships

In constructive living, we don't work on "relationships." Such an amorphous, abstract concept evades our efforts for improvement. We work on specific acts in concrete situations with particular persons. Nevertheless, it is possible to offer some general suggestions that can be applied in explicit ways in real life.

## SEEKING

One young man at a workshop voiced a rather common problem. Whenever he tried to generate a girlfriend, he felt tense. When he asked someone out on a date or even engaged an attractive woman in conversation, he felt uncomfortably awkward. Of course, such feelings are natural. They stem from wanting to be liked, wanting to avoid failure and, perhaps, from some recognition of his own self-centered desires. When he can shift his purposes from exclusive focus on satisfying his own needs to learning more about other people, serving others, and exchanging information, much of his tension will evaporate.

The dilemma is rather like that of overcoming neurosis. As long as one's main purpose is curing neurosis, then all activities are directed toward that purpose and cure remains elusive. The self-centered nature of the goal focuses more attention on the self,

DAVID K. REYNOLDS

with accompanying self-consciousness and discomfort. When goals shift to external issues and self-giving tasks, then relief is a natural result.

Rather than seeking a girlfriend in places (like singles' bars) where such a search is the overt purpose, I recommend doing volunteer work or attending adult-education classes. People working together toward a common purpose are naturally drawn together by their shared effort. Moreover, the service and learning in these settings result whether a suitable partner appears or not. Clear, straight purposes often produce indirect desirable side benefits. Self-serving purposes are difficult to achieve and usually have fewer side benefits.

## SEX

Sex is a way to merge oneself with another person, to disappear in the twosome that is one. But sex is also a way to separate oneself from another person, to draw a boundary that proclaims difference.

The why of sex is critical here. It affects the how and when and where of it.

But sometimes, in the act itself, a new why emerges and the me is lost or found, softened or hardened, put away or presented for inspection.

Then the world glows or glares.

## MARRIAGE

We seem to need a dependable circumstance like marriage in which to share intimacy. But I recommend to my students preparations for single life. I suggest that they develop the skills for creating their own friends, protecting their own health, supporting themselves financially and emotionally. Then they come to another person with strength and not with the hope of rescue.

Don't be obsessed about anything, even marriage. Marriage

offers no salvation, no security, no easy escape from self-centeredness.

Courtship is a time for creating compatibility, not merely discovering it. Through the acts of dating, gift giving, kind words, and intimacy the couple creates itself as a unit. Shared purposes emerge to draw the couple close together.

The successful marriage is sustained by mutual service and a blurring of roles. Each says to the other, "You are more important than what others say I should be." It seems to be important for husbands and wives to play together. The play is part of the general aim of creating a past together, creating an identity as a couple.

It isn't necessarily the case that "a family that prays together stays together." But it is true that a family with shared purposes, purposes larger than the individual members' personal dreams, has a superior chance of staying together. Constructive living recommends the goal of being reality-centered as one such larger purpose.

# Science and Reality

There was a time when I believed that taking in more information (reading more books, studying more social science, conducting more research) would solve our life problems. Now I'm not so sure. Either we already know enough or our ways of knowing are saturated or distorted or limited.

It seems more important at this stage to use, to apply, what little we already know. Then, if new ways of knowing open up naturally, if new insights blossom spontaneously, we can explore them, too. But now is the time for life practice and not the time for a single-minded, exclusive search for more intellectual information.

My doctorate is in anthropology, the study of humans. And most of my academic research has been in the discipline of psychology, the study of the human mind and behavior. But for all the years of study and research, I don't understand humans well at all. Half the human race is female. There were times in my youth when I thought I understood women, but I learned otherwise. I am a representative of the other half of the human race, males. I don't understand myself well, either. The male with whom I should be most familiar I cannot understand well. Since I cannot understand humans well (and others, including noted scholars, are no different), I am stuck with accepting what I cannot understand. Accepting is not so bad. Humans are, after all, the way they are. Whether I like myself and others the way we are, reality is what it is. Whether I understand myself and others the way we are, reality is what it is. Whatever parts of reality I want to work on to change, it is important to recognize and accept what exists now. To pretend reality were otherwise is not productive or honest.

In sum, then, it seems important for me to get on with living even though my understanding is terribly imperfect, even though reality doesn't meet my standards of ideal perfection, even though I am a flawed creature unsuited for easy accomplishment of many of the tasks I have set for myself. What else can I do but accept what is and work to change it?

### SCIENCE AND PURPOSE

When a scientific experiment is conducted, we can learn something whether the experiment turns out as expected or not. In either case, the results teach us something. Scientists create ways to ask reality to teach them. Our lives are much the same. When we have the attitude that success or failure (i.e., results as expected/hoped for or not) will teach us something, then failure isn't so dreadful. We can dare to risk, because one kind of success is assured. We can be confident that reality will teach us something based on our actions.

The image of scientists in white lab coats experimenting with esoterica far removed from reality is inappropriate. Scientists are merely performing a formalized, structured version of what we must all do, act so that reality can teach us something. Imagination and study can teach us what the results of our actions might be, but only action will demonstrate the results that reality presents to us.

# East and West

In a recent issue of *Seikatsu no Hakken,* the Moritist magazine with the largest circulation in Japan (over five thousand copies per month), advice is offered a wife and mother who suffers from severe anxiety. In rough translation, the advice begins: "Because the important thing is straightening out your daily life, think of your husband and children first and put yourself after them." As I read these words, I was struck again about the adaptations we have made in importing Morita's ideas to the West. It is natural to appeal to a woman's self-sacrifice in the Japanese cultural context, but we must also point out the benefits to the individual student (or client, if you prefer) in our ordinary practice of Morita therapy in the West.

Perhaps most Japanese recognize that when they fulfill their social obligations and responsibilities, they feel better about themselves. Perhaps many Westerners recognize the blows to satisfaction and self-image when they default on carrying their share of society's load. In any case, in the West we explicitly point out the benefits to the individual of changing to a more constructive life-style.

Although I may believe that serving others is the same as serving myself, although I may personally blur the distinction between altruism and self-gain, I find it helpful to begin my explanation of Morita's lifeway to my students in terms of its effectiveness in relieving their immediate misery. After all, relief from suffering of some sort is what they come seeking. So I must begin by teaching them techniques of constructive distraction and waiting for feelings to pass while keeping active. At some later stage we will see that cleaning a closet is important because the closet needs cleaning and not merely as a temporary distraction from symptoms. I shall point out that observing reality (including other people) is important in itself. It is a means of discovering what needs doing next and is not merely a means of getting one's mind off one's suffering. And the student's attitude will shift from merely waiting for unpleasant feelings to pass to the acceptance of whatever feelings appear (without liking them) while emphasizing positive behavior.

Some Moritists in Japan these days talk about being feeling-centered versus being purpose-centered. I think there is a third possibility. It is being reality-centered. Suzuki Tomonori often calls our attention to the fact that Morita himself never used the phrase *mokuteki hon'i,* often translated "hold to your purpose" or "be purpose-centered." Morita used the phrase *jijitsu hon'i,* or "be reality-centered." Feeling-centered people are focused on themselves, on the workings of their mind. Purpose-centered people have a dual focus. The purposes are theirs in the same way that feelings are theirs, but the purposes lead them to be focused on the external world as well. Reality-centered people seem to make no great distinction between the internal world and the external world. A reality presents itself; it contains feelings and hopes and ambitions and toothbrushes and mops and cars and salaries and neighbors. That ever-changing reality must be accepted while one works to affect it. There is no confrontation between me and this reality. I am as much a part of it as the keys on this keyboard. I am; it is; we are the way we are; we are part of the whole.

Morita wrote that his method is not religion but that it forms the groundwork for religion. It points to the solid ground of reality from which any genuine religion springs. Beyond the immediate relief from my suffering now, beyond the incessant preoccupation with me and getting my share, beyond me, there is something worth experiencing here. Can you see it?

DAVID K. REYNOLDS

# Meaningful Life Therapy

(In slightly revised form, parts of this chapter appeared in the journal *Culture, Medicine and Psychiatry* 13 [4]: 457–463, 1989.)

At Shibata Hospital, a few miles from the Shinkansen (bullet train) station at Kurashiki, a revolution in the care of cancer patients is beginning in Japan. Along with the usual surgical, radiation, and chemotherapy treatments for cancer, a new kind of psychotherapeutic technique is being utilized. It is called meaningful-life therapy, or *ikigai ryoho* in Japanese. The information for this brief report was drawn from interviews with pioneers of meaningful-life therapy, a visit to Shibata Hospital, two videotapes, and various issues of the newsletter *Ikigai Tsushin*.

Jinro Itami, a physician at Shibata Hospital, is the originator of this new technique. He has skillfully pulled together psychological techniques from several cultures and molded them into an auxiliary method of cancer treatment, with profound effects on the lives of cancer patients. Let's consider the theory, the practice, the values underlying meaningful-life therapy and a brief history of the method.

Much of the psychological theory underlying this method is explicitly borrowed from Moritist thought. Dying patients, too, must consider what is best to do about feelings and what is best to do about behavior.

Feelings are seen as natural phenomena, welling up from character, personal history, and circumstances. Fear and anxiety about death are normal. Effort to eliminate fears associated with a cancer diagnosis, for example, is both useless and unnecessary. The more one tries to escape from anxiety, the more one focuses on it and the stronger it becomes.

In Japanese the word *shi* is a homophone for both "death" and the number four. Many Japanese won't serve four food items on a plate or give a set of four objects as a gift. In order to avoid any associations with death, there are no rooms in Japanese hotels and hospitals numbered four. There are a variety of customs aimed at avoiding even indirect mention of death in social discourse in Japan. But meaningful-life therapy's theory points out that there are benefits associated with our fear of death as well. Death forces us to look at life. We take measures to preserve our safety, we use our limited time well, we may give up unhealthy habits (such as smoking) at least in part because we fear dying. The fear of death is uncomfortable, but it is both natural and beneficial. A potential problem lies not in the dread of cancer or of dying but in being so obsessed with the fear that one doesn't live constructively, fully, until death occurs.

Thus, obsessive fear of cancer and dying can be seen as a kind of neurotic reaction to the circumstances of illness. To some degree we all suffer unnecessarily from our worries and obsessions, but some people seem to take life's blows harder than others. Early Morita theory held that certain personality variables increase the probability of neurotic suffering in these circumstances. Persistence/obsessiveness, a general tendency to worry, strong physical and social needs, introversion, self-centeredness, and dependency contribute to increased neurotic suffering. Therapy must aim not at overcoming the fears, but at overcoming the negative aspects of these characteristics of the moment. Depending on the circumstances of life, these traits may have positive or negative effects. But when a person is faced with a terminal illness, his neurotic tendencies must not be allowed to interfere with constructive behavior within the genuine limits imposed by the illness. Western constructive living emphasizes the changeableness of humans rather than more static views of the person (e.g., personality traits).

The theory of meaningful-life therapy holds that it is in control over our behavior that hope lies. In spite of our fears, in spite of our personality traits, we can take responsibility for what we do in the time remaining to us. The terminally ill patient is encouraged to behave in ways that turn focus away from ruminations, toward achieving purposes, observing and participating in external reality, and being useful to others. In the doing of constructive activities a kind of life purpose is discovered. Notice that one need not (and, ordinarily, does not) *first* create some life purposes through reflection or introspection and *then* act to achieve them. In the actions themselves we construct our life purposes.

The cancer patients move from 1) private suffering to 2) recognition that others are suffering and fighting their cancer, too, to 3) acceptance of the reality of the illness and the fight that must be carried on to 4) an ability to live fully and deeply within the realistic limits imposed by the illness. In time, the patients come to see that their efforts not only combat their personal experience of illness but that they have impact on the larger society (other patients come to know of their fight and take hope), on the medical profession (physicians have more confidence in the strength of patients and begin to inform them of cancer diagnoses—telling patients of their cancer diagnoses is still uncommon today in Japan), and on the social sciences (new understandings of human psychological and social potentials become possible). The patients can make a contribution to others while making efforts to prolong and improve the quality of their own lives. Their final days take on increased life meaning. Again, we encounter the theme of acceptance of reality, an acceptance that carries no association of passivity. Accept cancer and fight it; accept one's limits and stretch them.

The orientation toward death can be summarized in a four-part outline: 1) we must accept the inevitability of dying; 2) it is impossible to eliminate our basic dread of death; we must live alongside it; 3) behind our fear of death is the strong desire to live life fully, realistically; 4) our fear need not pressure us unnecessarily; we can live each day doing well what needs to be done.

## PRACTICE

The emphasis is on group training and activities. Summer-study camps are offered for patients and their families. Exhibitions of the arts and crafts of cancer patients are held twice a year in Japan. Certainly the most celebrated media event associated with meaningful-life therapy was the assault on Mount Fuji by a group of ten cancer patients and their twenty-person support group in 1984. The preparations for and climbing of Mount Fuji in the rain provided a worthy purpose and a symbolic event well covered by press and television throughout Japan. Another group climbed Mont Blanc in Switzerland in 1987.

Meaningful-life therapy also includes a visualizing meditative technique adapted from yoga, zazen, autogenic training, and Simonton's visualization technique. This meditation is carried out two or three times a day, for ten to fifteen minutes at a time. Benefits are said to be greatest when practiced on rising and just before going to bed.

A low-stimulus environment is recommended, with low light and quiet. The patient is advised to go to the bathroom beforehand and to refrain from eating a heavy meal. Clothes are loosened. The exercises can be carried out while lying on the floor or sitting in a chair.

Each set of exercises begins with preparation of the environ-

DAVID K. REYNOLDS

ment, preparation of the clothing and posture, and some preliminary relaxation exercises. These preliminary exercises involve tensing and relaxing muscle groups and ten breaths with long, quiet exhalations. Then begins the set of meditative exercises proper.

Formal exercises focus successively on total relaxation, heavy hands, warm hands, a warm abdomen, and a cool forehead. Then comes visualization of the *rimpakyu* cells vigorously eating up the soft conglomerates of cancer cells. Visualization is enhanced, during craft periods, by crayon drawings of the destruction of the cancer cells. Finally several termination exercises, including stretching of arms and spine, deep breaths, opening eyes and rising, finish each set of meditations. Then the set of meditations proper is begun again. The cycle is repeated for about ten or fifteen minutes, two or three times a day as noted above.

Other meaningful-life-therapy activities include a year-end party, a marathon event, the exhibition of arts and crafts each spring and fall, various lectures, a summer camp, educational events for health professionals, a clearinghouse for phone and mail contacts among cancer patients, media coverage of the potential and problems of cancer patients, and a variety of opportunities for cancer patients to get together and learn about constructive living in spite of their illnesses.

VALUES

The values underlying this approach to cancer treatment are worth consideration. They include a value that illness brings some loss but also some possibility of gain. The compacted life of the terminally ill patient can be rich and constructive just because of the knowledge of approaching death. Special insights become possible. Standards and priorities can be reassessed.

Another value involves fighting with the illness. One may be a patient, but one need not be a victim defeated by the cancer. While accepting the reality of themselves with their fears and limits, the patients continue to do battle with their illness. They are encouraged to make efforts not to be defeated by their illness.

There is a strong desire to leave behind something for others. Shibata Hospital provides resident cancer patients the opportunity to visit elderly bedridden patients, to counsel other terminally ill patients, and to do minor tasks around the hospital. The arts-and-crafts exhibitions provide another opportunity for leaving something behind. It is said that some cancer patients are remarkably prolific and dedicated in their production of artistic works.

Another value is the group emphasis of treatment. There is communal suffering and support in the various group activities. It is important not to suffer and die alone.

A positive value is placed on knowledge of one's disease. It is unusual for physicians and families in Japan to tell cancer patients the nature of their disease. Meaningful-life therapy has already done much to educate the medical profession about the positive effects of telling patients that they have cancer. At professional meetings and educational institutions, health professionals are exposed to numerous examples of meaningful-life-therapy patients who have benefited from knowledge of their cancer's existence.

Underlying all this is the recognition that all illness carries a psychological component and that certain illnesses respond to adjunctive psychological approaches—bronchial asthma and peptic ulcer, for example. Meaningful-life-therapy practitioners cite the March 30, 1985, *Lancet* article (Pettingale, et. al.) that suggests (based on a very small study sample) that psychological attitude may be an important prognostic factor in the survival of patients with breast cancer. However, whatever effect meaningful-life therapy has on extending the chronological lives of patients, its value for improving the quality of their lives seems unquestionable.

DAVID K. REYNOLDS

Something here can be said of the brief history of meaningful-life therapy. In 1981 one of Dr. Itami's cancer patients was a middle-aged housewife, Mrs. Kitaguchi. She was extremely frightened of dying. Itami saw that this fear was similar to the phobias of neurotic patients and decided to use a Moritist approach to deal with Mrs. Kitaguchi's anxiety. They agreed to study together a way to live constructively regardless of her fears. She was given Moritist literature to read. She began a diary of her daily activities. She began to clean the roadway in front of her house, picking up trash, and straightening slippers in the entranceway of the hospital. She joined a women's table-tennis team, gave lectures of her experiences to health groups, and joined community action groups. After her second operation, she counseled other patients and did chores for them. With all this activity, she felt less anxiety.

This approach was gradually introduced to other patients. In 1984 a formal organization was begun built around five principles: 1) you are your own chief healer; 2) today involve yourself in this hour's purpose; 3) become useful to others; 4) practice living with cancer and your fear of death: and 5) people inevitably die and are accepted into nature even as they resist. Prepare yourself to face death realistically and constructively.

The membership in the meaningful-life-therapy organization grew to 462 members by the fall of 1986. Of that number, 190 are cancer patients scattered from Hokkaido, in the north, to Okinawa, in the south of Japan. The membership can be expected to continue to grow, with local patient groups throughout Japan and a network of cooperating physicians and hospitals. The organizational structure is patterned somewhat after that of the Moritist organization, Seikatsu no Hakkenkai. By 1987 there was a chapter of meaningful-life therapy in Santa Fe, New Mexico, led by Robert Hillman, a psychiatrist, and Barbara Bogart, an oncologist.

Meaningful-life therapy consciously distinguishes itself from the hospice movement. Although there is clear value in hospice facilities for certain severely ill terminal patients, there are some important differences between Japanese hospices and meaningful-life therapy, which are outlined below.

Hospices tend to be religious in orientation and sponsorship; meaningful-life therapy is not. Hospices aim at producing a peaceful attitude toward death; meaningful-life therapy aims at observing one's fear of death realistically, fighting the disease, and living constructively until the end. Hospices offer care that produces a passive patient; meaningful-life therapy emphasizes the self-care aspect of treatment. Hospices may tell patients of the nature and progress of their illness; meaningful-life therapy emphasizes the patients' need and responsibility to develop their own knowledge about their illness. The average stay in hospices in Japan is forty days; meaningful-life therapy aims at longer lifespans, cure, or remittance. Hospices provide inpatient care; meaningful-life therapy emphasizes home living and support groups. Hospices try to eliminate struggle and ease human relationships; meaningful-life therapy recognizes the need for struggle in these circumstances of illness. Hospices consider the effects of a patient's illness on the patient, the family, and friends; meaningful-life therapy expands the consideration to include the effects on health professions and the larger society. Hospices offer terminal care; meaningful-life therapy offers a psychophysical treatment program as an adjunct to ordinary medical care.

COMMENT

The realistic and practical orientation of meaningful-life therapy is worthy of note. It offers the possibility of constructive living and hope for extended living in tragic circumstances of severe illness. It is quite possible that a similar program could find acceptance in the West. For more information, write to Dr. Jinro Itami, 2-1-16 Hama no Chaya, Kurashiki-shi, 710 Japan.

The approach of constructive living is phenomenological. It takes reality as we perceive it. So it doesn't deal directly with death per se, although constructive living has much to teach about

DAVID K. REYNOLDS

dying. We continue to live as we are dying. Dying is a special kind of living. But death is only an abstraction for us. We can't experience it and report about it, despite the claims of life-beyond-lifers. Death is something we talk about, like society or culture or chemical events. None of these concepts exists out there in the real world. All are ideas humans have invented to talk about other ideas.

Death exists, to be sure. But our own death lies outside the possibility of our subjective experience. We shall die, but we won't experience death in the same way we experience a stroll in the park or a pain in the chest.

The beauty of meaningful-life therapy isn't that it extends life (that probability still hasn't been satisfactorily demonstrated) but that it makes meaningful, constructive living possible even in the difficult circumstances of chronic and terminal illness.

Death is natural. Death is necessary. We can prepare for death. We can acknowledge death. But for all our faith and under-standing and preparations, death can be terrifying. And that's all right.

Our bodies resist death. Our minds rebel against thinking about it much. We, like all living things, have a built-in drive to survive. Why should we find it natural to be open and accepting of death? Isn't it better to be open and accepting of *any* feelings that accompany our thinking about death? Isn't it more practical to struggle with death when we oppose it and welcome it when we embrace it? Why must we generate some appropriate, approved feeling concerning it? How could we do so even if it were the proper thing to do?

I have asked my students to discover how much direct control they have over their feelings. They discover that they have none. Neither they nor I can will feelings to appear or disappear on com-mand. Feelings concerning death are no different.

Life brings us many kinds of deaths. It is a kind of death when our classmates marry and move and we lose contact with them. Our parents and acquaintances die. Some of our dreams and plans for the future die. We lose some of our physical strength and abilities as we grow old. Our thoughts die and are replaced by new ones. Our hair and fingernails die. Pets and plants die. We live surrounded by death. Just look around; you can see it. All living things exist with death all around them.

Death has some element of sadness and loss and fear. But it also makes some wonderful, positive contributions to our lives. By knowing death we know the value of life. By knowing death we remember to use our lives well, to use the time we have to be alive. On the other side of the fear of death is the gratitude for living. The greater the fear, the greater the gratitude when we are saved from death. The greater the fear, the more determination we can have to live life fully.

I have lived with young people who thought death was a distant thing, not relevant to their lives. They wasted much time and felt no particular gratitude to be alive. I have lived with old American soldiers with terminal illnesses. They lived close to death. Some of them used their time thoughtfully, well; they were grateful to be alive.

As part of my training of people in constructive living in the United States, I ask them to write their eulogies (what will be said about them at their funeral), obituaries (what will be in the newspaper at their death), and epitaphs (what will be written on their gravestone). Then I ask them to imagine in great detail their lives from now until they die. Recently, I ask them what they want to be their final words as they die. These assignments aim at helping my students think about what they want to do before they die. How can they accomplish these goals? What needs to be done today?

I am not surprised that meaningful-life therapy is helpful for neurotic people, too. Neurosis is self-centered and narrow. It limits living. There is so little we do in our neurotic moments. Serious illness and death remind us that our time is limited. We cannot afford the luxury of neurosis. Furthermore, we can see the constructive lives of other meaningful-life-therapy members. It is possible to live well even in difficult conditions. We become inspired to use our lives fully.

DAVID K. REYNOLDS

I am very pleased to have a small part in the development and spread of meaningful-life therapy. I, too, shall die. Perhaps sooner than I expect. The time I have invested in meaningful-life therapy has been meaningful and worthwhile to me. I know that meaningful-life therapy will continue to provide valuable experiences to many people. We are all dying, after all; we must keep living fully to the very end.

# PART II

## CONSTRUCTIVE-LIVING PRACTICE

Here is the heart of constructive living. In the daily doing, the principles are mastered. The *taiken*, or experiential knowledge gained through action, is dependable and functional whether or not we can articulate the principles with verbal eloquence.

# *Exercises*

Notice that I never suggest that when you feel ready, you should continue with an exercise. It would be proper to advise that when you judge yourself ready, you should continue with an exercise. Judging takes into consideration feelings but also information about our tendencies to be lazy and timid, the benefits of the exercise, and our need to do it.

1. Said Hassanzadeh demonstrated for me the teaching value of a wood stove. In the morning, it requires careful preparation in order to get it going. "You can't just throw in the wood," he explained.

Said also pointed out that it is necessary to wear gloves when working with the hot stove and rough wood. That's like using an umbrella when it's raining. There is nothing admirable about enduring pain that could be readily avoided.

If you have a wood stove, you have probably learned its lessons. See if there are new ones to learn. Next time you build a campfire or light your barbecue, pay attention to what they have to teach you.

Life keeps on teaching us when we are open to learning.

2. Keith Johnstone* uses a technique in which he has his stu-

*1979, p.13.

dents march around naming with the "wrong" name whatever their eyes fall upon. They often experience a fresh, vivid perception of colors and objects after a few minutes of this conscious disconnecting of verbal labeling.

3. Practice silent action. Try to wash dishes as silently as possible. Cook a meal with minimal noise. Work on your car or your house with attention to decreasing the usual clamor.

4. Pause before a meal and list twenty of the people who made the meal possible. Eat the meal in silence. With each bite, silently thank one of the people on the list until all twenty people have been considered and thanked. (Adapted from an exercise devised by Gregg Krech.)

5. Interview a couple of people over sixty-five years old. Ask about the details of their lives. Of what are they most proud? What did they plan to do in their lives but never get around to doing? What are their hopes and plans for the future? What did you learn from them about yourself?

6. Take a homemade snack or sack lunch for someone you don't know well at the office or at school or in the neighborhood.

7. The next time you feel down in the dumps, call someone and don't mention a word about your own misery. Find out how that person is doing. Find out if there is anything you can do for him or her. Thank the person for talking with you. Go on to what needs doing next.

8. Greet a mailman, a truck driver, a tollbooth operator, a waitress, a crossing guard. Smile and compliment him or her on something specific.

9. Write your will. Consider not only what material objects you will leave behind but also what nonmaterial traces will remain.

10. When you die, what words do you want on your lips? Apart from the natural "I don't want to die" or "Thank you," what final sentence would you leave with each of your loved ones? What could you do today to live out that sentence for them?

11. Jogging the memory. Take "memory stimulating pills"—they may contain any ingredients whatsoever, but you must remember to take one every day.

12. Philip Saperstein came up with this sipping water exercise. With each sip thank someone or something for his or her contribution in producing this particular water.

# Koans

The following koans, or Zen-like puzzles, are presented without explanation, so that the constructive-living student can work on them without the distraction of knowing the answer beforehand. Each koan contains at least one constructive-living principle. I suggest that you ponder them one at a time and write out the single correct response to each one. Write some wrong responses to the koans, too, and know what makes those responses incorrect.

### KOANS FROM AMERICAN CONSTRUCTIVE LIVING

How can I get rid of my anxiety?
>Throw it out.
>But I'm too anxious to throw it out.
>Then squeeze it out.

Life comes at me so fast; how can I handle it?
>Round things are round, blue things are blue.
>But—
>And resistance is resistance.

I used to sit still in one position without moving whenever my favorite football team was winning.

DAVID K. REYNOLDS

Now I watch the game.

He went on vacation and came back a different man.
She closed her desk drawer and became a different woman.

Echoes heard from reality's mirrors—what are they?

I have trouble getting along with others.
Would you have a seat, please.
Sure. Especially I have trouble accepting authority.
Excuse me just a moment. Ah, yes. Where were we?
I was saying . . .

But what if there *were* such things as past lives?
Close your eyes. Notice how dark it becomes. Open your
eyes. What do you see?

Each time you feel shy, it is a new shyness.

Look for the single source of your thoughts, your feelings, your
choices.

## ZEN KOANS APPLICABLE TO CONSTRUCTIVE LIVING

Last year's poverty was not real poverty, but this year's poverty is
poverty indeed. (Miura and Sasaki, 1965)

The deer hunter doesn't see the mountains, the miser doesn't see
men. (Miura and Sasaki, 1965)

When an ordinary man attains knowledge he is a sage; when a
sage attains understanding he is an ordinary man. (Miura and
Sasaki, 1965)

Master Ummon said, "The world is so wide, why at the chime of
the bell do you choose to put on a monk's garment?" (Hoffman,
1975)

Hokoji pointed to the clouds in the sky and said, "All these lovely snowflakes do not fall on any particular place." (Hoffman, 1975)

Master Haku-un said to Master Hoen, "Once there came a few guests from Mt. Ro. Every one of them was enlightened. When they said something it was perfect. When asked about a koan, they understood it . . . But that is still not enough." (Hoffman, 1975)

DAVID K. REYNOLDS

# *Maxims*

Recent maxims from constructive-living trainees include:

I thought so is not so; I do so is so.

> —Nathanael Birk

To do or not to do; what is your purpose?

> —Rod Hoeltzel

Talk is cheap; doing is priceless.
I do, therefore I am.

> —Mel Clark

There is no confidence without competence.

> —Joyce Boaz

Easy does it, but do it.

> —Patricia Ryan

Practice *is* perfect.

—Katherine Bean

Own this moment, and this moment . . . and you own all time.

—Ron Madson

When you pass a mirror, notice its frame.

—Crilly Butler

Suffering is the Breakfast of Champions.

—Greg Ottinger

Seen on a bumper sticker:
   No matter where you go, there you are again.

Other constructive-living maxims:

   Tragedy's triumphs and suffering's satisfactions.

Can anything good come from tragedy and suffering? When I consider the leadership of the constructive-living movement, there are divorces, deaths, alcoholism, experiences of abuse as a child, even survival of a loved one's murder in the reality of our pasts.

Teaching is self-negation.

We teachers would sometimes like to talk about ourselves, but we must listen to our students' difficulties. We must take on the identities of our students in order to teach them effectively.

Putting me outside me.

Attention to reality puts me outside me. We lose ourselves in our situations as we lose ourselves in a book. When someone talks to us, we become that person. Issues of taking time out or resting disappear—who is resting? That is not to say we don't rest. Of course we do. But the resting takes place naturally, as genuinely needed, without being considered a particularly noteworthy issue.

The other side of the beautiful source.

In the book *Constructive Living,* there is a maxim about finding the positive need or desire underlying any symptom. When you can find the beautiful source in yourself, you can find it in others. Of equal importance, when you can find the beautiful source in others you can find it in yourself. There's no important difference.

Reality, the only show in town. Now playing.

Constructive living is about learning to play our parts in this grand show.

# PART III

## CONSTRUCTIVE-LIVING TALES

The tales in this section were written in order to teach some con-structive-living truths to my students. I suggest that you read each story without looking at the comment, then think about the mean-ing and purpose of the story for a while. You might even put aside the book for a day and come back to the story a few times as you recall it. Then reread the story along with the comment and go on to the next story.

*Waves*

Not so long ago, in a hazy hot summertime, kids camped in cabins by a mountain lake. In the evenings one lad sat on the bank and threw stones into the lake. He was trying to stop the rippling waves of the lake with his stones. He succeeded only in creating more waves than before. Still, he held on to the infinitesimal possibility that one stone, properly placed and timed, would cancel out the interacting wave forces on the lake and create a moment of waveless peace.

Across the lake, in another camp, a stereo began to blare. The lad rushed back to his cabin and turned up his stereo in an attempt to drown out the music from across the way. His head throbbed when the blasts from both stereo systems combined into sonic pulses magnified beyond the decibel capabilities of either system.

Dinner tasted terrible because the cook put too much salt in the stew, then tried to cover up his mistake with sugar and pepper. After dinner the lad leaped into his bunk bed and pulled the covers up over his head. He was, it seems, afraid of the dark.

And he tried to convince himself he was having a great time in camp. Under the coarse wool blanket, he forced a smile with tears in his eyes.

*Too often we go to extremes to oppose or demolish something that could be accepted and incorporated into our lives.*

# *Parting Gift*

Their father was dying of cancer. He went about it in a determined but not-so-painful manner. Week by week he showed less appetite. He lost weight, weakened, and slowed the watchspring of his life.

The family was closer then than it had ever been. Their father was dying for them, in a sense. They had a special purpose in coming together then. They shared experiences and strategies for keeping him comfortable and satisfied during his last days. They opened up to one another about their future hopes and fears. They made plans for their eventual deaths.

The old man's terminal illness was a farewell gift to his family. He left them something new as he took something old away. He paid a tremendous price for that gift. They appreciated the cost.

*Dying restricts some opportunities while opening the doors to new possibilities. Minus and plus, give and take, always change, only change.*

**DAVID K. REYNOLDS**

# Butterflying

It's tough being a butterfly. Life is short. Rain beats down on your delicate wings. Winds blow and make flying next to impossible. Plenty of creatures consider you to be a colorful, tasty morsel. Humans see you as a collectible pest.

Swaying flowers make landings difficult. Mates are scattered and fluttering about in this madly shifting world.

It isn't easy at all, you know.

Nothing is *solid*. Just bits of pollen and tastes of nectar and shifting breezes and a sun that won't stay put. All that change gets you to wondering . . .

Before the Big Change, there were solid branches for crawling and substantial leaves for chewing. My many feet were solidly attached to home, and my pace was regally slow.

Now it's here and there, always on the move.

Can't go back, though. Can you?

*The butterfly is noted for its Big Change. But life holds only change for all of us. As butterflies, we see more of the world than we saw before. The wind blows us to new heights and new perspectives.*

# *Conversation*

"What do you do?" he asked.

    "I listen; I teach," was the reply.

    "You listen? What kind of work is that?"

    "Just listening."

    "People pay you to *listen?*"

    "Don't you think listening is worth something?"

    "Well, I never thought of it that way . . ."

    "That is what I do. I listen; I teach. Just now."

    "Just now?"

    "Yes."

    "Oh, I see."

    "Thank you."

    "You are an unusual person."

    "Thank you."

*Good teaching often involves helping students see the limitations of their questions. Looking at our questions helps us see the boundaries we have drawn in our lives.*

DAVID K. REYNOLDS

*Fame*

Henry Fonda died yesterday.

So did Mr. Swenson, the old man who lived downstairs in this building.

Mr. Swenson's death didn't make the papers.

*Will yours? Will mine? Does it matter? Perhaps Mr. Swenson knows.*

*Clearly, it matters how we live until we die. Living well is not-dying in every sense.*

# Diamond Misery

Once upon a puzzling time, people evaluated the value of their contacts with others in terms of how much they suffered when those contacts ended. When Floppy's boyfriend broke up with her, she was certain that he hadn't been very important to her because she didn't feel terribly terrible. When Floppy's brother, Flippy, faced the death of his aunt Val, he didn't grieve much, so he decided that he hadn't been close to his aunt. All that seemed to make some sense.

Then, when Floppy's father died and she was sad but not all broken up, Floppy didn't know what to think. She *had* been close to her father. Nevertheless, she seemed to be able to go about her daily life without collapsing, and she only cried once. Others wondered why she didn't hurt more. Floppy herself wondered. Had there been some hidden grudge against her father? Was she stunted emotionally in some way to be unable to recognize and express her overwhelming grief?

Floppy's mother was upset with her for not falling apart. Her social world certainly expected more tears. Perhaps they considered her a cold, unfeeling bitch, or so Floppy worried.

It wasn't that Floppy was fighting against her grief. She welcomed it; she wanted more of it. Thus, she could confirm her deep love for her father. But feelings are intransigent critters—they

DAVID K. REYNOLDS

don't go away when we want them to, and they don't appear on cue, either.

Floppy found herself pressured to fake more misery than she really felt. Then she got confused about which was real and which was artifice. Then she got confused about who was feeling this mixed bag of feelings.

After a long time, Floppy figured out that it makes more sense to value folks while you are with them than to try to compute their worth to you after they are gone. And the grieving comes when it will.

*This story includes the restatement of a familiar theme—feelings are uncontrollable directly by the will. They are best accepted as they are. They provide information, but they are not the measure of our lives.*

## Body Parts

Once upon a distant time, people made love by giving up some part of their bodies to their lovers. Everyone possessed leather bags into which their mates placed some part of their bodies as they made love. A fingernail or strand of hair, an eyelash or a bit of skin were commonly exchanged. But it was not uncommon to hear of fingers or ears or a whole arm or leg being slipped into a bag in moments of great love or great passion. There were even a few stories of lovers who actually climbed into the leather bags and disappeared, literally swept away by their emotions.

The donated body parts sometimes rejuvenated miraculously, but sometimes they didn't. In the latter case, people carried for life the handicap evoked by their love. Of course, those who climbed into the leather bags of another never emerged again. It was commonly thought that such people were reborn, perhaps as a family member of their lovers.

In those days the phrases "giving yourself to your lover" and "making sacrifices for love" were taken quite literally.

*What do those phrases mean today?*

DAVID K. REYNOLDS

# Beautification

There was a man who drilled (by hand) small holes in concrete streets and sidewalks and planted (again, by hand) flower seeds in them. Then he watered them and heaven watered them and, in time, others watered them (sometimes unknowingly).

Some flowers burst out, bloomed, and brought life to the cities. In spite of tires and high heels and boots and carbon monoxide, the flowers bloomed. And they kept on blooming, because that is what flowers do. They continue to bloom, over and over again, in spite of tires and high heels and cigarette butts and noxious gases. They bloom. In spite of . . . flowers . . . bloom.

*And, of course, so do people. So does love. So does hope.*
*Watch out for the trucks!*

# *Freeway*

Shark tow trucks cruised through the school of rush-hour traffic. Minnow cars flitted from lane to lane seeking the perfect slot. Mr. Shattuck found himself behind a creeper. As usual. Or so he considered his circumstance.

Why me? Why do the turtles always appear right in front of me? He berated fate for his invariably bad fortune.

The freeway branched ahead. Cars began combing their way through the lanes toward the freeway exit. Shattuck saw his moment and sliced his way into a vacated slot in the fast lane. Just ahead of him, the turtle had done the same. Oh no!

He's the sludge of humanity, thought Shattuck. He has no consideration for anyone but himself. Why do they give guys like that driver's licenses? In his eyes, the turtle's taillights became devilish faces distorted into sneers. The brake lights flashed, appearing discolored and blotchy.

Ahead, the driver of the turtle was thumping his palm against the wheel. Why didn't the guy ahead of him move any faster? And now there was a sucker driving too close on his tail. Tap the brakes with the left foot while holding down the accelerator. Just enough to flash the brake lights and give the guy back there a scare. That's right! Shook him up a bit! Why do all the crazy drivers gather around me? This traffic is one big headache.

DAVID K. REYNOLDS

*   *   *

*Those who appear to be turtles may wish to be rabbits. Some turkeys wish to soar like eagles. When do I know enough about their circumstances, their reality, to make a judgment about them?*

# Runaway

Lisa Squirrel twitched her bushy tail in the air a couple of times and raced in a series of small *m*'s for the nearest pine tree. The velvet mountain heat didn't bother her. She loved the shadow wind that breathed caresses through her fur. Above, only vibrating needles and rolling whiteness.

But Lisa Squirrel wasn't appreciating her forest home today. She faced a pine-sized problem. She sat on a branch high up and watched the scrub oaks across the way overflow and dribble down the mountain. Her eyes followed suit, overflowing with warm tears. Her male friend, Ricky Squirrel, was showing signs of losing interest. And the only solution Lisa could come up with was to dump him before he got around to dumping her. He was a bit slow for Lisa anyway, and his eyes wandered too much. Still, she would miss him.

On the Angeles Crest Highway nearby, huge trucks lumbered past like obese matrons heading for another cocktail. Harold pulled his car from the end of the parade onto a turnout and exited. The world seemed to be sliding past at forty-five miles per hour. He felt that he skated rather than walked away from the car. Exhaustion forced his eyelids open. They would no longer close, yet he felt himself slipping into sleep with eyes wide open. Sleep, he realized, is a state of giving up one's mind. It has nothing to do with the body at all, he thought.

**DAVID K. REYNOLDS**

Harold was moving on to (hopefully) better things before the boss back in Pasadena realized that he had given Harold too much responsibility on the job. Harold had maneuvered a transfer through the main office. Denver would be a welcome change. Southern California was due to fall into the ocean anyway, wasn't it? He leaned back against the trunk of a pine and dozed.

Overhead, the United flight to Newark carried Clara back to Mom and Dad. Five months of college had been enough. Bill was a nice guy, but being around him was like being fed by an ant. No matter what its will and effort might be, the results are insufficient. Better to bail out before the loneliness deepened in that arid land so far away from home.

Who knows what might happen?

*In life you have to break in your own shoes. Some people try to do that by running away.*

## She Ought to Want to Try Again

Once there was a triangle that longed to be a circle. Now, most triangles are quite stable forms, but they aren't good at rolling around the world like circles. The triangle could see that life seemed to go more smoothly for circles; their lives seemed to be—how shall I put it?—well rounded. But filling out its sides and blunting its points are big steps for a triangle. Your typical triangle treads tediously through the torturous trenches of time. That rat-a-tat-tat sound epitomizes the movement of a triangle contrasted with the sliding, smooth sweep of the symmetrical and shapely circle.

Actually, becoming a circle is not nearly as difficult as the triangle anticipated. After all, the necessary lines are there already. It's just a matter of reshaping. The reshaping makes the circle. Again, the process of reshaping makes the circle.

*Jennifer owes love and care to her elderly mother. After all, her mother provided love and care to Jennifer for years. That's basic. Jennifer forgets sometimes, in the midst of feeling responsible, that she naturally loves and cares for her mother. She likes to do so, at least most of the time.*

DAVID  K.  REYNOLDS

*Jennifer ought to lose weight. So she has decided. Diligently, she exercises. Jennifer hardly ever notices that she enjoys exercising, at least most of the time. With her eye on the far goal of weight loss, Jennifer stumbles through the underbrush alongside the trail.*

*Her job is interesting and meaningful. But Jennifer is obsessed with the necessity of working for a living. She has to go to work each workday. She must earn that paycheck. Work is work. Play is play. Life experiences that are enjoyable must come during leisure hours.*

*Jennifer believes that someday she will change her life; someday she will change her whole attitude toward her existence. Someday something will happen to her, someone will come along, some revelation will strike. In the meantime, she'll get along somehow. Change is frightening . . . even when it's delightful.*

# *Train Trip*

The first drops of rain darted down the train window, leaving sharp pencil-thin tracks. The fan slurred fuzzy warm air on his body already slick with sweat. The neon light above zummed. He sat with no shirt on, only a *hara maki* waistband around his middle. Protect your *hara,* your belly, they told him, no stomach problems then. We even use *hara maki* on babies. Does it work because they believe it works? he wondered. But babies don't believe it works.

*Sachikimo-koton, sachikimo-koton, sachikimo-koton, koton, koton.* The train drummed its rhythm into his thoughts. After a while it stopped at a small station, Tagi, to wait six minutes while another train passed in the opposite direction. At this station the single track divided briefly into two.

The young Japanese woman in the seat across from him sat lost in travel dreams of a young man who would be alike her enough to fit yet different enough to create a lifetime of interesting reminiscence. How predictable the world has become, he mused. In America and in Japan young people stimulate each other, middle-aged people admire each other, and old people wait for each other (to cross a street, to board a bus, to die). Each group is isolated from the other by walled space and years of unique experiences. Outside the train ranks of trees marched down the mountainside.

**DAVID K. REYNOLDS**

The express heading south flashed past. Windows rattled and ears throbbed. Then, after another wait, the train got underway again. The track led upward. Through the gray afternoon wetness he could glimpse valley after valley opening into the winding crease along which the train moved with effortful patience. He wished to explore some of those valleys at leisure someday. The contortions of rock, the crevasses, the spires, the concealing foliage—all are worth noting in detail. All reveal something more than geography. The broad leaves of the taro plant mirror a collective reflection.

The next station was fairly large, a popular spa. The waiting room there was filled with those-who-wait. Wood benches and molded plastic chairs. In-between moments—people living in futures of what will be and memories of what was. A few of them were brushing through the sliding present scenes with awareness and relish, savoring the greetings and partings. Backpacks propped against a pillar. Gifts wrapped in *furoshiki* scarf bundles. The hum of interplaying casts of characters.

He sat alone now, watching through the train window. A few of those in the waiting room sat alone, too, and seemed comfortable with their aloneness. Others were alone but seemed anxious, incomplete by themselves yet fearful of the approach of anyone else.

Who am I to be observing and commenting on all this? he mused. But then, that is my way. I don't hold myself above these others. I am among them, one of them, yet apart. There is no need to travel far in order to watch truth in its reality dance. It is always right here, now.


*It's in the eyes, in the seeing. Reality, truth, wisdom, gratitude. Not right in front of your eyes. In your eyes. Is your eyes.*

# Eartrip

Lynnette thought she had been invited to Millie's house to tell Millie about her recent trip to Canada. But Millie seemed more interested in telling Lynnette about *her* trip to Canada a few years ago. Millie asked just enough questions to be polite and to generate prompts for her own tales.

That evening Lynnette attended a banquet with her husband. She felt guilty that she didn't generate much conversation around the banquet table. With all the high-powered minds around her, it seemed safer to listen. Anyway, by the time she thought up something clever to say, the conversation had moved on to other areas.

Strangely Millie, as well as the guests sitting near Lynnette at the banquet, seemed to have a good time even though Lynnette mostly listened. They seemed to appreciate her company even though she didn't produce a lot of conversation. In fact, if you asked them, you would discover that these folks found Lynnette to be one of their favorite people to be around. She was a great audience.

Lynnette felt guilty sometimes that she wasn't as quick with words as some others. She wished she could deliver sharp repartee at will. Someday perhaps she would take a course or something. In the meantime, she may discover that she has a

DAVID K. REYNOLDS

good ear for the music of speaking, and that, too, is a wonderful gift.

*Until we develop the talents we desire through the discipline of effort, we may appreciate the talents we already have.*

## Especially Ordinary

Once upon an urban time, there was a spiritual master who watched video, ate frozen foods, and drove a pickup truck. Very few people recognized him as a spiritual master because he wore no robes, he ate meat, and he was constantly tinkering with a straight-eight engine that resisted efforts to keep it running. What business would a spiritual master have with grease all over his hands?

A few kids in the neighborhood recognized that there was something special about Hank. (His name was another liability in the spiritual circus circuit—not exotic at all.) He didn't swear when he dropped the hammer on his foot; he just picked it up and went back to pounding. He explained what he was repairing to even the greenest young mechanic. His garage workshop seemed tidier than most. And the only time the kids ever saw him in a rush was when a grinder motor caught fire, and then he had the extinguisher chemical all over it before anyone had time to get scared.

Kids noticed that people came by to visit Hank every now and then. A few wore fancy suits and looked like insurance-company executives or bankers. Most, however, dressed simply, perhaps a bit on the drab side, or so it looked to the youngsters. Hank would stop what he was doing—watering or working on the truck or patching up the house or digging in the garden or lounging in the

DAVID K. REYNOLDS

hammock—and he and his visitor would disappear in the house for an hour or two. Then they would come out and shake hands and Hank would stand and watch the visitor drive off until he or she was out of sight. Then he would just pick up right where he left off.

Another peculiarity about Hank was that he would stop what he was doing and listen to whatever any kid had to say about anything for as long as the kid wanted to talk. Now *that* kind of adult is as rare as they come. New kids in the neighborhood seemed starved for such attention. They took advantage of Hank's listening ears for what seemed to them long periods of time. And Hank never seemed to tire of listening and asking questions. But there were baseball games and trap-door spiders and skateboards calling. In time the new kids, too, came around only when they had something they thought important enough to ask or tell Hank.

No temple, no beard, no mystical symbols. There was a television antenna on the roof and empty frozen-dinner containers in his trash sometimes. Admittedly, Hank did wear sandals on hot summer days. To the kids and (apparently) to the visitors, Hank was a special person. To the parents of the young people in the neighborhood, Hank was a nice guy, an ordinary guy. He wasn't particularly wealthy or famous or successful; certainly, he was no saint. After all . . .

*Constructive living provides a life strategy for becoming ordinary. We fear that we are not ordinary (neurotic) and we yearn to be not ordinary (superior). Constructive living teaches us how to be natural, just ourselves, nothing special. Disappointed? You expected more? Perhaps there is consolation in the truth that being nothing special, in the sense used here, is a state both rewarding and difficult to achieve.*

*For the marvel, the special quality, is in this moment, in this unique circumstance, not in you or me. I am just a part of this moment, an aspect, a participant. I am just ordinary, but this reality is ever-changing wonder!*

# The Mind

Swirling patterns, wreathes of mist emerging from nowhere, fading, fading. The cauldron stirred by the old monk gave off just such fumes. Steam appeared a few inches above the surface of the bubbling liquid as though its connection was tenuous or not at all. At times the monk would grasp at a wisp of steam, perhaps seeking some tangible quality in it. But always it escaped through his clenched fingers and reappeared above them, re-forming into new designs. Dynamic. Motion.

There was a time when the monk was an artist. In those days he held glass above the cauldron. Then the hot vapors etched patterns on the glass. He sold his works of art in galleries. His unique creations made him famous and reasonably well-to-do. But the etched glass was static. It showed only what happened in that moment, then. It was the motion itself, not the swirlprints, that held fascination for him.

For a time he retired from his craft and tried to generate the swirling patterns just by imagining them. But they settled and became stereotyped as he lay on his couch. He was bored.

So he returned to the activity of his cauldron, but he no longer produced the etched-glass artworks. Rather, he invited in friends now and again to watch the vapors rise as he stirred the pot.

\* \* \*

DAVID K. REYNOLDS

While viewing the broad vista from a cliff in the Catskills, I remarked to my students that out there were their minds in two senses (by analogy and by content). And bird thoughts flew up in two senses (again, by analogy and content).

"Watch the thoughts arise and fly away like the birds," I told them. "Watch the mist thoughts, listen to the crows' cawing thoughts. They arise and disappear."

All of them. All of us. Like vapors.

## Glossy Revenge

Brenda was hurt by her first boyfriend. He used her and left her for someone else. Brenda decided on the basis of that experience that men aren't trustworthy. Moreover, she decided that they need to be punished. She felt a strange fascination about these male creatures who could cause her such pain and cause her to seek revenge.

She found that she could attract men, study them, then get her revenge by dumping them just as they became hopeful and eager to share her bed.

"I'm not the kind of person who just climbs into bed with anyone. I'm a good person, a religious person. I have standards and deeper desires than merely the physical." Thus, she justified her vengeance. And she climbed into bed with no one.

Brenda sometimes wondered why she worked so hard at staying attractive and coyly seductive. But then, when one has a part to play, one must dress for the role.

*There is winning in losing and losing in winning.*

*The Japanese put it somewhat differently. "Makeru ga kachi,"* *they say. Losing is winning.*

# Narrow Bridge

Between the Japanese land called ChuRaku and the country called Jiyu there was a narrow bridge, Shuyo, over the Kanjo River.

Travelers across the bridge were few. The steep steps leading up to the suspended track intimidated all but the hardiest of wayfarers. Those who traveled with lots of bulky luggage saw that they couldn't pass over the bridge with so many possessions. So most people decided to ford the river or buy a ticket on some sort of ferry. Ferry boats were notoriously unscheduled, and they offered no guarantee that travelers would reach the opposite shore. Still, the captains of these ferries reaped great profits from their association with the Kanjo River.

Those who tried to ford it found that the Kanjo River is swift and deep in places. The footing is treacherous across small mossy stones. Over the years, ropes have been stretched across the river so that travelers can hold on as they make their laborious way to the other side. Nevertheless, each year many are swept downstream by the current.

Quiet pools in the lee of huge boulders tempt some people into the river. But the pools are always adjacent to raging currents. There is no peaceful crossing of that river. Those who are washed away by the flow must get to the near shore and trudge back upstream to the Shuyo Bridge. They may have an easier time of crossing the bridge the next time around, because they lost many of their possessions to the river. But the bridge remains narrow and intimidating.

The legendary land of Jiyu turns out to be different from what most travelers expect. After they make the difficult crossing of the river, the travelers encounter a land not so different from their previous homeland. Far from being a land of milk and honey, Jiyu has the same craggy barren wastelands mixed with lush jungles and plowed fields as ChuRaku. Furthermore, there are thousands of difficult river crossings within the land of Jiyu. However, the crossing of the bridge changes the travelers somehow so that they see their new home with new eyes. Their feet are tougher and their hearts are more open to the beauty that presents itself to them. Not a single one of them longs to return to ChuRaku.

Looking down from the bridge into the raging torrent is awe-inspiring and terrifying. The spray hits the traveler's face and blurs the vision. It wets the planks and makes them slippery. Inch by painful inch, the traveler moves toward the land of Jiyu.

*We move toward freedom across a bridge of self-discipline over a river of feelings.*

DAVID K. REYNOLDS

# How the Elephant Got Its Trunk

Once upon a time, a long time ago, even before Freud, there lived a strange creature called Elephant. Now this creature was strange indeed because it had a big body, big feet, big ears, and a tiny nose. Furthermore, Elephant had a serious problem. It lived in morbid fear of Tiger. Elephant was so afraid that it no longer went to the local watering hole for fear of being pounced upon by Tiger. Lately it had become so bad that Elephant hardly dared to peek its conspicuous head out from behind its favorite boulder. As you might imagine, Elephant was having a pretty hard time accomplishing any of its usual elephantine chores. Elephant was getting more miserable each day.

Then one day, as though out of nowhere, a large balding monkey who called himself Mr. Erectus appeared right next to Elephant's boulder.

"Hey, Elephant," he called. "Why is a big creature like you hiding behind this boulder?"

"Well, sir," Elephant explained, "I'm always afraid that a mean, hungry Tiger is going to pounce down on me. I just can't come out."

With a knowing smile, the balding one said to Elephant, "Look at your nose. I bet you never realized that you could see your nose, small as it is, anytime you wanted."

"Why, you are right!" cried the astonished Elephant.

"Furthermore, I bet that while you have been paying attention to your nose, you forgot all about the mean, hungry Tiger."

"You are right again!"

"Look," said Mr. Erectus. "It is natural to be afraid of Tiger. Most of your jungle friends are. I don't exactly hang out with Tiger myself. However, you may not realize that you can feel afraid and still get on with your elephantine responsibilities. Always recall that when you were looking at your nose with full attention, you were not noticing any feeling of fear. Pretty soon you will realize that you can live a full elephantine life despite felinophobia."

In the days and weeks that followed, Elephant experimented with paying full attention to its nose. It ventured out from behind its boulder. It was still pretty scared at times, but Elephant realized that to be scared sometimes is natural. Before very long Elephant was down at the water hole carousing with the impalas.

In the meantime, a curious thing had happened. With all that attention, Elephant's nose had been growing longer and longer, little by little, until it was eight feet long. Elephant discovered that this nose was a most incredibly useful thing. It could be used to pick up grass, give showers, and even to trumpet warning if Tiger came near.

Many years later, Elephant came across a creature who looked an awful lot like that helpful Mr. Erectus, except this fellow was even more bald and wore khaki skins.

"Say, you're not the Mr. Erectus I met long ago, are you?"

"No, I'm known around here as Mr. Sapien."

Mr. Sapien took a long, careful look at Elephant. Then he asked cryptically, "Have you ever tried balancing on two legs?"

"No, I never have," replied Elephant.

"Well, if you are willing,"—Mr. Sapien grinned—"I could make you a star overnight!"

"Really?" exclaimed the excited Elephant.

"Sure. All you have to do is come along with me and Tiger to the big top in the city."

DAVID K. REYNOLDS

*This fine tale was written by Brad Robinson, a physician who completed the Morita-guidance-certification course on Maui. It is used with his permission. Some of our deepest fears look foolish to others. Sometimes when we accept those fears as natural and get on with living constructively, new opportunities open up for us.*

## Who's That?

In a far-off dusty land there lived a very old man who suffered from a disease that affected his mind. He forgot things easily, and he didn't recognize himself in the mirror.

He lived in a special hospital for old people. Every day he got up and went to the washroom to wash his face. There was a long line of washbasins and a long line of mirrors in the washroom. As the old man walked past each mirror, he waved to the person he saw reflected in it. He wanted to be friendly with those people in the mirrors. He didn't know that he was waving at himself. The mirror images waved back. The old man felt happy that he got along so well with his new friends.

*Many of my students don't or won't acknowledge their reflection in reality's mirror. Hopefully, someday they will come to make friends with the honest images that reality reflects to them.*

DAVID K. REYNOLDS

## Pride or Confidence?

Sasha was the daughter of a toy maker in a land far away. When she was in her teens, she was selected to become a lady-in-waiting at the palace of Queen Sola. Sasha considered herself merely the daughter of a common merchant. She felt no confidence to become a direct servant of the queen. Her first years in the palace were sheer misery.

One day, when she was at home on vacation, she stood at the kitchen table making pies with her mother.

"You certainly work long hours at the palace," her mother said as she laid the thin strips of pie crust over the apple filling.

"I don't mind the hours so much. It's just that I don't feel like I belong in the palace. So many of the other people there were born into nobility or at least grew up in the shadow of the palace. We are just ordinary merchants. I'm not fit to serve the queen." Sasha pinched the circumference of her pie circle.

"Of course you are," her mother reassured her. "You are my daughter and good enough for any task. But frankly, I think I would be just as uncomfortable as you if I stood in your shoes. Fancy places make me feel strange. I'm much happier quietly working in the kitchen or in the shop."

"Me too," replied Sasha. "I guess I'm just not cut out to be in the palace."

"In a way I'm relieved that you don't feel at home there." Her mother placed the finished pies in the oven. "I wouldn't want you to get all puffed up with pride living around those high-class people. You might forget your roots; you might forget your family."

"You never have to worry about that. I just can't feel at ease around all that luxury and power." Sasha began washing the mixing bowl.

Ten years passed. Sasha and her mother were baking a fresh batch of pies in the same kitchen.

"Another new dress? We'll have to build you a new room to fit all your clothes in." Her mother smiled.

"It's part of the job, Mother. The queen doesn't want to see the same old clothes all the time. And I have my eye on a knight."

"A knight? Heavens! My daughter eyeing nobility? You certainly have changed."

"Not so awfully much. Really. You get used to the palace, just like you get used to a toy shop. It takes time. And now I fit in there as well as anyone. But I'm still your daughter, and—" She paused, smiling. "I'm still the *second*-best pie maker in the neighborhood."

"Well, it looks as though I lost a pie-making assistant but I gained a very classy, confident pie maker."

They laughed together.


*What is the difference between confidence and pride?*

*The word* pride *is used in at least a couple of ways in English. I was taught to avoid pride because it is self-centered, unbecoming, and "goeth before a fall." I was also taught to take pride in myself and pride in my work.*

*Similarly, confidence was supposed to be necessary for success, but overconfidence was dangerous and to be avoided.*

*In constructive living, we place our confidence in reality. We let feelings of self-confidence and pride in self come and go as they will. We keep steadily about doing the best we can, whatever reality sends for us to do. Like Sasha, we are likely to find self-*

confidence growing as we stick it out in uncomfortable situations. We learn to do well in spite of our urge to flee at the slightest sign of discomfort. Self-confidence, then, becomes some sort of experience-based memory of our past successes in rough times.

However, the greater confidence, the more dependable confidence, is reality confidence. Reality steadily teaches us about itself again and again, with infinite patience. We can trust reality even when we feel no self-confidence.

# Lonely Star

Once upon an intergalactic time, a star burst with great energy and brightness. It was just at the time when the forces of the universe swept other heavenly bodies close to this newly gleaming star. So all the universe seemed to take notice of its wonderful glow.

At first the star considered itself something special. It could see its reflected brightness in other celestial spheres. It was right up there with the brightest of them. With time, however, the star began to notice that its reflections on the faces of planets and stars were distorted. They weren't receiving the true light on all wavelengths. It was as though they created their own images of its luminous output. They didn't see the shining star's real colors.

They don't really know and love me, the star reflected sadly. They each have some false image of me. Would they like me if they could see what I truly am?

About that time, clouds of interstellar gas swept through the universe. There were long centuries in which the star's light couldn't be seen by others. The contrast between basking in reflected glow (however distorted) and dark isolation turned the star's thoughts inward. It realized that, in some sense, it had been more at peace with itself when it was just another ordinary light in the firmament. Its sudden rise to flame created new glory but also

DAVID K. REYNOLDS

new desires and greater swings in its polarity of mood. It felt lonely now when alone.

The star recognized that its fiery brilliance couldn't be turned off so that it could return to its former state. Once the atomic furnaces yield their energy, the reaction cannot be suppressed. They must burn until they are exhausted of energy.

What a wonderful/terrible dilemma. The star had it all and wanted still more. More centuries down the line, when the brilliance had diminished somewhat, would the desires diminish, too? Would the star try to husband its dwindling resources? Would it aim for a final flash or a steady glow?

*The television hostess had been on soaps before. Now she interviewed her television guests quickly, professionally. When the cameras came on, she became alive, alert and poised in a special way. I could see and feel the change in her. I wanted to tell her that she could be alive when the stage lights were off, too.*

# References

Akegarasu, Haya. *Shout of Buddha,* trans. Gyoko Saito and Joan Sweany. Chicago: Orchid Press, 1977.

Aoki, Shigehisa. *Morita Masatake Sensei no Kotoba (The Words of Masatake Morita).* Tokyo: Seikatsu no Hakkenkai Morita Therapy Series, 1976.

Fujita, C. *Morita Therapy.* New York: Igaku Shoin, 1986.

Hoffman, Yoel. *The Sound of the One Hand.* New York: Basic Books, 1975.

Ishiyama, F. I. "A Case of Severe Test Anxiety Treated by Morita Therapy." *Canadian Counsellor* 17 (4), 172–174, 1983.

Ishiyama, F. I. "Morita Therapy: Its Basic Features and Cognitive Intervention for Anxiety Treatment." *Psychotherapy* 23 (3), 375–381, 1986.

Ishiyama, F. I. "Positive Reinterpretation of Fear of Death: a Japanese (Morita) Psychotherapy Approach to Anxiety Treatment." *Psychotherapy* 23 (4), 556–562, 1986.

Ishiyama, F. I. "Use of Morita Therapy in Shyness Counseling in the West: Promoting Clients' Self-acceptance and Action Taking." *Journal of Counseling and Development* 65, 547–551, 1987.

Iwai, H., and Reynolds, D. K. "Morita Therapy: The Views from the West." *American Journal of Psychiatry* 126 (7), 1031–1036, 1970.

Jeffers, Susan. *Feel the Fear and Do It Anyway.* New York: Harcourt, 1987.

Johnstone, Keith. *Impro: Improvisation and the Theatre.* New York: Theatre Arts Books, 1979.

Kondo, A. "Morita Therapy: a Japanese Therapy for Neurosis." *American Journal of Psychoanalysis* 13, 31–37, 1953.

Kora, T., and Ohara, K. "Morita Therapy." *Psychology Today* 6 (10), 63–68, 1973.

Kora, T. "Morita Therapy." *International Journal of Psychiatry* 1 (4), 611–640, 1965.

Kubose, Gyomay. *Zen Koans*. Chicago: Regnery, 1973.

McGee, Richard K. "Review." *Contemporary Psychology* 31 (10), 750–751, 1986.

Miura, Isshu, and Sasaki, Ruth Fuller. *The Zen Koan*. New York: Harcourt, Brace and World, 1965.

Morita, S. *Seishin Ryoho Kogi (Lectures on Psychotherapy)*. Tokyo: Hakuyosha, 1983.

Murase, T. "Naikan Therapy." In *Japanese Culture and Behavior*, eds. T. Lebra and W. Lebra. Honolulu: University Press of Hawaii, 1974.

Ohara, K., and Reynolds, D. K. "Changing Methods in Morita Psychotherapy." *International Journal of Social Psychiatry* 14 (4), 305–310, 1968.

Pettingale, Keith W., et al. "Mental Attitudes to Cancer: an Additional Prognostic Factor." *Lancet*, March 30, 1985.

Phillips, Lakin. *A Guide for Therapists and Patients to Short-Term Psychotherapy*. Springfield, Illinois: Charles C. Thomas, 1985.

Reynolds, D. K. *Morita Psychotherapy*. (English, Japanese, and Spanish editions) Berkeley: University of California Press, 1976.

Reynolds, D. K. "Naikan Therapy—an Experiential View." *International Journal of Social Psychiatry* 23 (4), 252–264, 1977.

Reynolds, D. K. *The Quiet Therapies*. Honolulu: University of Hawaii Press, 1980.

Reynolds, D. K. "Morita Psychotherapy." In *Handbook of Innovative Psychotherapies*, ed. R. Corsini. New York: Wiley, 1981.

Reynolds, D. K. "Naikan Therapy." In *Handbook of Innovative Psychotherapies*, ed. R. Corsini. New York: Wiley, 1981.

Reynolds, D. K. *Naikan Psychotherapy: Meditation for Self Development*. Chicago: University of Chicago Press, 1983.

Reynolds, D. K. *Constructive Living*. Honolulu: University of Hawaii Press, 1984.

Reynolds, D. K. *Playing Ball on Running Water*. New York: Morrow, 1984.

Reynolds, D. K. *Even in Summer the Ice Doesn't Melt*. New York: Morrow, 1986.

Reynolds, D. K. *Water Bears No Scars*. New York: Morrow, 1987.

Reynolds, D. K. *Flowing Bridges, Quiet Waters*. Albany: SUNY Press, 1989.

Reynolds, D. K. *Pools of Lodging for the Moon*. New York: Morrow, 1989.

Reynolds, D. K., and Kiefer, C. W. "Cultural Adaptability as an Attribute of Therapies: the Case of Morita Psychotherapy." *Culture, Medicine, and Psychiatry* 1, 395–412, 1977.

Reynolds, D. K., and Yamamoto, J. "East Meets West: Moritist and Freudian Psychotherapies." *Science and Psychoanalysis* 1, 187–193, 1972.

Reynolds, D. K., and Yamamoto, J. "Morita Psychotherapy in Japan." In *Current Psychiatric Therapies*, ed. Jules Masserman, 13, 219–227, 1973.

Shibayama, Z. *A Flower Does Not Talk*, trans. Sumiko Kudo. Rutland, Vermont: Tuttle, 1970.

Simonton, O., and Mathews-Simonton, S. *Getting Well Again*. Los Angeles: Tarcher, 1978.

Soseki, Natsume. *And Then*, trans. Norma M. Field. New York: Putnam's, 1978.

Suzuki, T., and Suzuki, R. "Morita Therapy." In *Psychosomatic Medicine*, eds. E. D. Wittkower and H. Warnes. New York: Harper and Row, 1977.

Suzuki, T., and Suzuki, R. "The Effectiveness of Inpatient Morita Therapy." *Psychiatric Quarterly* 53 (3), 201–213, 1981.

Takeuchi, K. "On Naikan." *Psychologia* 8, 2–8, 1965.

Thich Nhat Hanh. *Being Peace*. Berkeley: Parallax, 1987.

Wolfe, Gene. *The Island of Dr. Death and Other Stories*. New York: Pocket, 1980.

For information about the nearest Constructive Living instruction
and Constructive Living group programs, call:

| | |
|---|---|
| New York State | (914) 255-3918 |
| New York City | (212) 472-7925 |
| Washington, D.C. | (703) 892-4174 |
| Los Angeles | (213) 389-4088 |
| Chicago | (708) 234-9394 |
| Cleveland | (216) 321-0442 |
| San Francisco | (415) 584-0626 |

or contact Dr. Reynolds:
Constructive Living
P.O. Box 85
Coos Bay, Oregon 97420
(503) 269-5591

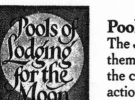